The Dogo Argentino

Dogo Argentino Facts & Information: Dogo Argentino Temperament, Breeders, Dog Price, Adoption, Breed Standard, Weight, Health, Rescue, and More

Julie Walker & Lois Diaz

Copyright © 2015

Copyright and Trademarks

All rights reserved. No part of this ebook may be reproduced or transferred in any form or by any means without written permission of the publisher and author. This publication is Copyright Protected (2015) by Ocean Blue Publishing. All products, publications, software and services mentioned in this publication are protected by trademarks.

Disclaimer and Legal Notice

This product is not legal, accounting, medical or health advice and should not be interpreted in that manner. You need to do your own due-diligence to determine if the content of this product is right for you and your pets. While we have tried our very best to verify the information in this publication, neither the author, publisher nor the affiliates assume any responsibility for errors, omissions or contrary interpretation of the subject matter herein.

We have no control over the nature, content and availability of the web sites, products or sources listed in this book. The inclusion of any web site links does not necessarily imply a recommendation or endorsement of the views expressed within them. Ocean Blue Publishing and the author take no responsibility nor will they be liable for the websites or content being unavailable or removed.

The advice and strategies contained herein may not be suitable for every individual or animal/pet. The author and publisher shall not be liable for any loss incurred as a consequence of the use and or the application, directly or indirectly, of any information presented in this work. This publication is designed to provide information in regard to the subject matter covered.

Neither the author nor the publisher assume any responsibility for any errors or omissions, nor do they represent or warrant that the information, ideas, plans, actions, suggestions and methods of operation contained herein is in all cases true, accurate, appropriate, or legal. It is the reader's responsibility to consult with an appropriate professional advisor before putting any of the enclosed information, ideas, or practices written in this ebook in to practice.

Acknowledgements

With grateful thanks to the many Dogo Argentino admirers out there who own or would like to own this wonderful dog. It is you that helped this book to go from being an idea to becoming a reality.

Thank you to the many dog breeders that have provided insights into breeding and raising dogs over the years. Without your commitment, we would have no pedigree dogs today.

Thank You.

"I still remember as if it were yesterday ... the day when my brother Antonio told me for the first time his idea of creating a new breed of dog for big game, for which he was going to take advantage of the extraordinary braveness of the Fighting Dog of Cordoba. Mixing them with other breeds which would give them height, a good sense of smell, speed, hunting instinct and, more than anything else deprive them of that fighting eagerness against other dogs, which made them useless for social group hunting. A mix that would turn them into sociable dogs, capable of living in freedom, in families and on estates, keeping the great courage of the primitive breed, but applied to a useful and noble end; sport hunting and vermin control."

- Dr. Agustin Nores Martinez

Table of Contents

Chapter One: Introduction 5

Chapter Two: Understanding the Dogo Argentino 8

Chapter Three: The Personality of the Dogo Argentino 18

Chapter Four: Finding a Dogo Argentino 21

Chapter Five: Getting Ready for your Puppy 32

Chapter Six: Bringing your Puppy Home 44

Chapter Seven: Caring for your Dogo Argentino 56

Chapter Eight: Socializing your Dogo Argentino 62

Chapter Nine: Training your Dogo Argentino 69

Chapter Ten: Feeding your Dogo Argentino 89

Chapter Eleven: Dogo Argentino Health 104

Chapter Twelve: Breeding your Dogo Argentino 127

Chapter Thirteen: Saying Goodbye to your Dogo Argentino 151

Chapter Fourteen: Common Terms 155

Chapter Fifteen: Resources 174

Chapter 1: Introduction

Chapter One: Introduction

Chapter 1: Introduction

The Dogo Argentino, or Argentinian Mastiff, is a very large dog that was bred to be sociable around people and especially children. At the same time these muscular white dogs were bred to have good social group traits so they could work as big game hunters in their native Argentina, hunting wild boar and the local mountain lions (called puma), rather than hunting independently. They are at their best when hunting with people and other dogs rather than alone.

Strong, intelligent, and with the quick reflexes of an athlete, these large white dogs have short hair and stand 60 to 65 cm (23.6 to 25.6 inches) for females and 60 to 68 cm (23.6 to 26.8 inches) for males and weigh 34 to 45 kg (75 to 100 pounds).

Their temperament makes them well adapted to defending their human companions, to police and military work, to search and rescue, and to training as service dogs. Yet the Dogo is prized because the breed is also a wonderful family dog. Dogo Argentino clubs and associations are found from Caracas to Cairo and beyond.

The breed originated in Argentina as a result of the efforts of Dr. Antonio Nores Martinez who bred together a male Cordoba fighting dog and a female Bull Terrier and then bred the offspring with other breeds and strains as will be explained below.

The choice of a male Cordoba fighting dog, essentially a Mastiff, was to create a hunting dog but to breed out the inherited tendency to fight. Martinez wanted dogs able to hunt in their social groups and to develop similar attachments to humans.

This brings up the importance of socializing the dog from its early puppy days around children so they recognize them and adults as valued members of their social and material world, providing play, comfort, and food.

This book will be beneficial to the many people interested in owning one of these remarkable dogs. More profile information is given in the following chapter, and the needs of the Dogo Argentino are explained

Chapter 1: Introduction

further, even down to effective ways of feeding puppies to make them cherish their relationships with people.

Common health problems of the Dogo Argentino are then considered, along with how to choose a puppy in a way which minimizes risks of adult health issues.

In the end, the breeding of the Dogo Argentino is considered in such a way as to produce that most glorious of all results – happy, healthy Dogo Argentino puppies.

Much of the experience and advice covered in this book comes from decades of personal experience with the breed. I am fortunate to be part of a family of Dogo breeders.

In the end, all the issues you need to consider and decisions you will have to make are touched upon, most of them from a number of perspectives.

We hope you enjoy learning about the Dogo Argentino and that this book will prepare you for finding and raising a happy, healthy dog.

Chapter Two: Understanding the Dogo Argentino

As with any animal, it's important to learn as much as possible before making any kind of purchase. This is extremely important when it comes to owning a dog. Dogs come in hundreds of different sizes, temperaments and breeds. Not only that, but a dog is a living, breathing, feeling creature who will depend on you for its every need. In many cases, you and your dog will spend 10 to 15 years together. So it's important to make a wise decision.

While a dog may look cute, some breeds do not fit with some owners. Breeds that are always on the go are not recommended for owners with limited mobility, while a laid back breed isn't recommended for owners who are active. Knowing the breed's traits before you bring home a puppy will ensure that the puppy is the right fit for you.

Which brings us to the Dogo Argentino. This large, powerful breed has a constantly growing population of fans as it becomes more well-

Chapter 2: Understanding the Dogo Argentino

known and recommended by current owners. But there is a lot that every dog lover should know about this breed before they make a purchase.

This chapter is designed just for that purpose and it will cover the history of the Dogo Argentino, the breed standard and finally some general facts about the breed.

What is a Dogo Argentino?

The Dogo Argentino is a large-sized, powerful breed of dog also known as the Argentinian Mastiff. These dogs are known for being loyal. They have been bred for hunting wild boar and other large game in their social groups, and will defend their family even unto death. This was the specific goal of Dr. Antonio Nores Martinez who first developed the breed in the 1920s, and later through decades of thoughtful breeding and cross-breeding.

"Dogo" means "bulldog." The original male dog used to create this new breed was a Cordoba Fighting Dog, from Cordoba, Argentina. The Cordoba Fighting Dog was not so much a single breed as it was a collection of cross-breeds and near breeds that were large enough to compete in the kinds of dog fights conducted at that time in Argentina.

The Cordoba Fighting Dog is extinct now, partly because these dogs were so aggressive that they would fight each other to the death. It is said that they would rather fight than mate. The initial bitch that was used to produce the Dogo Argentino was a Bull Terrier.

History of the Dogo Argentino

The history of this breed started with the dream of Antonio Nores Martinez. He dedicated his life to his passion, creating the first and only native breed of Argentina. Here you will find a basic overview of the foundation of the breed.

Chapter 2: Understanding the Dogo Argentino

Starting with the Cordoba Fighting Dog because of their bravery and other desirable qualities, Dr. Martinez mixed the dogs with other breeds to give his dogs greater height, a better sense of smell, greater speed, and hunting instinct.

Martinez was also determined to remove the aggression and eagerness to fight other dogs from the new breed he was creating. He wanted to do this so that his dogs could hunt together in their social groups without any aggression towards one another.

He wanted this new breed to be sociable, and able to live freely with their families and on estates. He wished for them to be courageous and above all, brave like their ancestors. He wanted them to use their courage for sport hunting and to control vermin as needed, instead of fighting each other.

Martinez crossbred the dogs that had the desired characteristics and excluded the ones that fought too much with other members of their social group, or that had other undesirable characteristics.

Breeds of dogs that were subsequently bred with the crossbred dogs Martinez was producing are said to have included Great Danes, Great Pyrenees, and the Dogue de Bordeaux. Other breeds that added to the Dogo Argentino included the Boxer, Spanish Mastiff, Pointer, and Irish Wolfhound.

The Dogo Argentino was accepted by the Argentine Kennel Club in 1964. It was accepted by the Fédération Cynologique Internationale (FCI) in 1973, thanks to the efforts of Dr. Agustin Nores Martinez, the brother of the breed's creator. It is the first and only Argentinian breed in the FCI. The breed was accepted into the AKC's Foundation Stock Service in 1996 and is currently in the Miscellaneous Class, awaiting entry into the Working Group.

Chapter 2: Understanding the Dogo Argentino

Breed Standard of the Dogo Argentino

The breed is recognized by ACA, ACR, AKC/FSS, APRI, BBC, DRA, FCA, FCI, NAPR and NKC. As with all breeds, the Dogo Argentino has a breed standard. In fact, it has slightly different breed standards in different countries and registries. What this means is that there is a set temperament, look, coloring and size of the breed that the dogs should conform to according to the registry that registers the dogs.

In general, the standard for the breed involves a height of 60 to 65 cm (23.6 to 25.6 inches) for females and 60 to 68 cm (23.6 to 26.8 inches) for males and weigh 34 to 45 kg (75 to 100 pounds).

The breed temperament is mild within its social group and with people, while being fierce when hunting in its group. This was the intended purpose of their creation, by Dr. Martinez and his family.

The most unusual breed trait is the upward lifting nose which adds a few centimeters to the height at which they are sniffing the scent of prey. That with their white coats, massive skulls, tall height, wide barrel chests, long powerful heads and clipped ears, signal the hallmarks of the breed. The ears, which are set high, are surgically clipped so prey cannot grab onto them with their teeth and tear them off. This also makes the dog look more challenging, forming small, erect triangles.

The overall build of the dog should be one of an athletic powerhouse which is nimble in the forest and comfortable at home. The thighs and shoulders have demanding musculature as does the neck and every element of the head. The neck has abundant skin which folds into wrinkles when the dog extends its head upwards.

The head should have a massive skull with the breed's very unusual concave orientation of the muzzle from the forehead to the nose. The nose lifts upward, is large and should be black. The teeth have a scissor orientated bite for tearing into the flesh of prey.

Chapter 2: Understanding the Dogo Argentino

The eyes of the Dogo Argentino should be brown or hazel, medium in size and be set apart with pink or black rims.

The tail of the Dogo Argentino is carried low and curves backwards towards its end.

Coloring

Dogo Argentinos are completely white bodied except that a large black spot over a single eye is allowed in some national and association standards.

Coat

The coat is thick and short, has no undercoat and sheds at a middling rate. Occasional brushing is necessary for good grooming and household hygiene as explained presently.

Size

The various local, national and international Dogo Argentino associations tend to agree that the standard involves a size of about 60-65 cm (23.6-25.6 inches) for females and 60-68 cm (23.6-26.8 inches) for males and weigh 34-45 kg (75-100 pounds) as mentioned previously.

Life Span

Dogo Argentinos live about ten to twelve years.

General Facts about the Dogo Argentino

While the breed standard helps you identify what the dog should look like, it doesn't really tell you a lot about the general facts relating to them. Before you purchase a Dogo Argentino, it's important to make sure you know what the breed is really like. You should know what to expect if you are considering living with this dog.

Chapter 2: Understanding the Dogo Argentino

How much do Dogo Argentinos shed?

The Dogo Argentino is an average shedder in most climates. Regular grooming when there seems to be extra dog hair about is sufficient to keep the house clear of it. Dogos are typically clean dogs that don't require much grooming. There are some that claim that they shed a lot but breeders believe otherwise.

Are they difficult to train?

All dogs can be difficult to train if they do not have a firm owner. It is important to train from a young age; especially with the Dogo Argentino which will look for a group leader in its social world, and try to take that role itself if there is no other human or animal doing so. It will do this from a young age.

In fact, some Dogo Argentino owner groups do not recommend them for people who have never owned and trained a dog before.

Dogos are very intelligent dogs and they have a strong desire to please. They do need an owner who is firm with them, but not harsh. They respond well to fair and positive training.

The general training skills of the owner are very important to future satisfaction in this relationship. We recommend puppy pre-school or puppy kindergarten classes for a Dogo Argentino and good socialization from a young age.

We also recommend that an owner and a young Dogo Argentino attend obedience classes together, especially if they are a first-time owner. The Dogo Argentino has a tendency to become an assertive dog and requires proper training. It's also important for the owner to understand training techniques and how to be in charge of their dog.

One early skill is to simply put the puppy on a leash and take long walks. It is not the romp at the dog park that fulfils the Dogo's deepest

Chapter 2: Understanding the Dogo Argentino

desires. It is long walks under the cue of the nearest leading being in its environment and this is you.

If you are not in charge of your Dogo Argentino, he will take charge, and he will do this from an early age. This is part of this breed's temperament and genetic inheritance. There will be a lot of discontent for both of you if the relationship begins to take on this pattern.

Your puppy will learn basic cues over time, but taking long walks together will satisfy and please him. On a leash there is no question who is ultimately the boss, but it is not the entire solution. This theme returns several times in various ways. You will be able to teach your puppy what he needs to know with classes, training, and the rules at home.

Are they good with children?

The Dogo Argentino does very well with children and tends to match his personality to the children in the house. Active children will mean an active Dogo Argentino while calm, quiet children will produce a calm, quiet dog. Dogos are fierce when hunting, but at home they are as gentle as any family pet. They love their family, especially children. Their human family is their social group and they are genetically programmed to seek and adapt to a social group. This was Dr. Martinez's great accomplishment in altering the temperament of a fighting dog and making it into a hunter and family companion.

If there are no children in the house it is important from a young age to arrange experiences with children for the Dogo. It is not wise to have what will become one of the world's most powerful dogs growing into adolescence with no experience around children.

They will become tolerant, affectionate and protective towards children if they have regular contact with them. It is much more difficult to achieve that result if training around children is delayed. However, if you don't have children yourself, you can take your Dogo puppy to the

Chapter 2: Understanding the Dogo Argentino

park or other places where children play and socialize him to play with children.

Are they good with other dogs?

Yes, the Dogo Argentino does very well with other dogs, especially if they are raised with them. They are generally social group-oriented and they are happy being with other canines. However they can be very dominant. Therefore, same-sex congeners, if intact, may be a challenge to be around.

Are they good with non-canine pets?

While they can be trained to be tolerant of cats and other small, non-canine pets, the Dogo Argentino does have a strong prey drive and may chase smaller animals. It's always best if a Dogo puppy is raised with your other pets so he will learn to accept them from a young age.

Do they make good watchdogs?

The Dogo Argentino is an alert breed that will watch their home and is rated as high in their ability to learn to do so properly. They make excellent watchdogs because they will bark alerts when they see something suspicious and their native ability to respond well to general watchdog training is very high.

However, the Dogo is not a nuisance barker. They don't bark a lot, just to hear themselves bark. If your dog is barking, it usually means there is something worth investigating.

In general, the Dogo Argentino is a cheerful, humble, friendly breed. They are reserved and suspicious around strangers, but they are very amiable and gentle at home. As with many other Mastiff-type breeds, they require good socialization from an early age so they will be more accepting of visitors when you invite them over.

Chapter 2: Understanding the Dogo Argentino

Do they do well in all climates?

The genes of the Dogo Argentino go back to where their ancestors were adapted, in some instances, to harsh winters. They do well in all climates. Make sure that regardless of your climate, your dog has proper shelter from the weather when they are outside, including shade and a breeze in the summer.

How much do they cost?

To purchase a Dogo Argentino, you should expect to pay between $500 and $4000 (£330 to £2630) with most being offered at $1500 to $3000 (£985 to £1970) in the United States. The cost depends on the history of its breeding and titles of parents and grandparents, whether it has been raised in a home environment, location of the seller and location of the buyer.

It is not recommended to have your Dogo delivered to you as it can be extremely stressful on the dog, although many do still opt for this method of delivery. Do note that shipping will add to the costs.

Other factors include whether the Dogo Argentino has been altered, whether its line has been bred for show or for a household pet, whether it is male or female, whether it is of a special line such as giant Dogo Argentinos, and other factors specific to individual countries.

Do Dogo Argentinos do well in apartments?

The Dogo Argentino literature is full of happy stories about the breed and apartment living. Of course they need to be out of doors regularly for exercise under the owner's supervision. If the Dogo doesn't get regular exercise, they can do terrible things to an apartment. Don't flatly dismiss the idea of bringing a Dogo Argentino to live in an apartment but don't fail to be realistic about its outdoor exercise and especially walking needs.

Chapter 2: Understanding the Dogo Argentino

The breed's instincts mean that long walks on a leash are especially important. Unsupervised exercise opportunities are great but it is the long walks on a leash that they crave, due to their social group instincts, and this establishes the owner as the leader of the social group and pacifies the Dogo Argentino.

Does the Dogo need a lot of exercise?

Yes, they do. You don't have to have your own yard, but you do need to be realistic about the amount of exercise these dogs require. They are large, athletic dogs. Long walks are great but they need extensive regular exercise to maintain their fitness and to be mentally and emotionally content.

The Dogo does have a strong prey drive so if you are walking your dog or taking him to a dog park, be aware that if he sees a squirrel, rabbit, or some other small game, run across your path, he may have the urge to pursue it. Make sure you have a tight hold of the leash when you walk your Dogo. Fences should be tall and sturdy to discourage the pursuit of game.

Is the Dogo Argentino a fighting dog?

No, the Dogo Argentino is *not* a fighting dog. In fact, the breed was specifically created to remove the fighting instincts through the breeds used to develop it.

However, the Dogo Argentino does look similar to some Pit Bulls. These dogs are not related in any way. The Dogo Argentino was developed to hunt big game animals and to be a family companion. Unfortunately, lawmakers often do not understand the difference and they have included the Dogo Argentino in some of the same bans that affect the Pit Bull and other fighting dogs.

Chapter 3: The Personality of the Dogo Argentino

Chapter Three: The Personality of the Dogo Argentino

Every individual Dogo Argentino is different but the breed's fame is justly earned when it comes to their even temperament and happy life within a family. This alert breed is always aware of the goings on around and in his home and they make excellent watchdogs.

The Dogo was and continues to be bred as a guardian, although this does not mean the dogs have a serious nature when they are in a home where their needs are being satisfied. The Dogo is energetic outdoors and tranquil indoors.

If your household is not active it will distress the Dogo Argentino over time. They are active dogs and they enjoy being with an active family. If there are to be cats, they should be there from the start. Kittens, for instance, should accompany the arrival of the Dogo, or adult cats

Chapter 3: The Personality of the Dogo Argentino

already present and higher in the pecking order, so that the Dogo puppy will accept them as more senior members of the social group. It is amusing to see the full grown Dogo Argentino still "obeying" such cats.

The Dogo's individual personality will range within their personality 'type,' but how the breed reacts, temperament-wise, has as much to do with how the dog is raised and trained as genetics. When we discuss personality, we often look at the general traits that we see in the breed. However, your Dogo Argentino may not have all of the same personality traits.

In general, a Dogo should not be made to live in a household with another Dogo Argentino or other kind of dog of the same sex. A lot of time will be lost trying to diffuse their attempts to decide who is boss. They usually get along best with members of the opposite sex.

When they bond with their owner, the Dogo Argentino is very outgoing. They are affectionate and love spending time with their family. They love physical contact such as cuddling up at their owner's feet.

The type of family does matter. While they can do very well with children, they need to be properly socialized to them. Always remind children how to properly handle a dog.

Non-canine pets can prove to be a challenge for the breed. If they are introduced at a young age, the breed can do okay with smaller non-canine pets such as cats. If they are not introduced when your Dogo is a puppy, you may have difficulties when bringing the new pet into the home because the breed has a high prey drive. If they are not properly trained, they may attack smaller, non-canine pets because they will not see them as members of the family social group.

And that brings us to the territorial temperament of the breed. They will fiercely protect their homes and yards so it is important to properly socialize them. They should be accepting of people and other animals

Chapter 3: The Personality of the Dogo Argentino

to help prevent territorial aggression in the dog. Socialization is essential to preventing this and we will discuss how to socialize your Dogo Argentino puppy later on.

When it comes to differences between the sexes, most owners find that there is a distinct difference in temperament. Males are generally more playful and they have a spunky personality.

Generally, males will rule the roost and will often try to be the more dominant creature in the home. They will mark their territory and they are usually more territorial than females. On the other hand, males are usually more inclined to accept new people and tend to be quite outgoing. Finally, males are often the more affectionate of the two.

Females, on the other hand, are usually more submissive than males. They are affectionate but it is not always a playful affection. They can be playful but most of the time, females tend to be reserved.

However, bear in mind that this is not a set rule. You can have a playful and outgoing female and a submissive and reserved male. A lot of your Dogo's temperament can depend on socialization and training.

In the end, you must start early with the proper knowledge to train your dog to respect you and obey you.

Chapter 4: Finding a Dogo Argentino

Chapter Four: Finding a Dogo Argentino

Finding a Dogo Argentino breeder is not particularly difficult. We have included a list of Dogo Argentino breeders in the Resources chapter later in the book to help you along. Finding a Dogo Argentino puppy for sale can be harder. In both the United States and the UK, this is a relatively rare breed.

These dogs are banned under the Dangerous Dogs Act in the UK and they are banned in some towns and cities in the United States. The breed is also banned in Ukraine, Iceland, Australia, New-Zealand and Singapore.

However, you can own a Dogo Argentino in most of the world. If you are looking for a puppy, you may get lucky and find one right away. If you don't find a Dogo Argentino puppy for sale immediately, or you don't find a breeder you like, don't give up. Keep checking with breeders and talking to them. Even if a breeder doesn't currently have a litter, they could be planning a litter in the next few months.

Knowing a good breeder puts you on the inside track to getting the puppy you want when one is available. Even with a popular breed like the Dogo Argentino, you may have to wait a little while to get the

Chapter 4: Finding a Dogo Argentino

puppy you want from a particular breeder. It's not unusual to be put on a waiting list for a pedigreed puppy in many breeds.

It's always important to talk to the breeder, not just to obtain information about the puppies, but to find out if this is a person you can trust.

Finding a breeder

Finding a Dogo Argentino breeder can be a difficult task because Dogo Argentinos are a rare breed. These dogs are popular in some places, despite the legal issues. You may have to travel to get one. This can be frustrating when you are excited about owning one, but the wait is worth it.

Some owners have managed to have their Dogo Argentino delivered through a home delivery service. We would not recommend this method of sourcing your Dogo Argentino, due to the stresses that are caused during travel. Not to mention that a decent breeder will be reluctant to ship a puppy.

In addition, you could be looking at a waiting list of up to two years before you have a puppy. This can be frustrating when you are excited but the wait is worth it.

We have compiled a list of breeders in the Resources section for your ease. This is a good place to start.

It is important to note that you should do your research on all of the breeders listed. The priorities of breeders can change and where one was excellent at one time, they may not be currently.

When you are looking for a breeder, it is important to look for the following attributes:

Chapter 4: Finding a Dogo Argentino

A breeder that will answer your questions

One of the first things to look for with regard to breeders is to look for one that will answer your questions. Yes, breeders can be very busy. Not only do most of them have full time jobs and family commitments but they may also have puppies they are caring for.

However, with that being said, the breeder should be open to discussing the breed with you and potentially owning a puppy. If it is all about putting in a deposit to hold a future puppy and nothing else, then you should choose a different breeder.

A breeder that is active with the breed club and kennel club

Not all breed clubs are created equal, and so if the breeder is affiliated with one, but not another - they could still offer you a high quality Dogo Argentino.

A few good questions to ask a breeder would be: Do your puppies show? How do they place? As the breeder, do you require a home check? If the answers to these questions are positive, then you are moving in the right direction. Also, it is normally a good sign if the breeder is initially distrusting.

A breeder that participates in activities with their dogs

Make sure your Dogo Argentino breeder is active with their dogs. They don't have to show, although that would be a good option. Ensure that they are doing more than simply placing their dogs in a kennel.

A breeder that can give you background checks on their dogs

Choose a breeder that knows the background of their dogs such as pedigree, health of the lines and where the dogs came from. The

Chapter 4: Finding a Dogo Argentino

breeder should also know the history of the breed and the breed standard.

If the breeder doesn't know much about the breed, then it is an indication that you should look elsewhere.

A breeder that has a puppy plan and health clearances

Look for a breeder that has a breeding plan for their overall kennel. Are they trying to breed a certain trait or just breeding for puppies. Do they have a puppy plan on how they are raised? Do they have health clearances on their dogs? Can they talk to you knowledgeably about socialization and temperament?

If the answer is no to one or more of those questions, choose a different breeder. Every litter should have a goal in mind that will improve the breed. In addition, they should have a plan as to how the puppies will be socialized and reared.

Finally, the breeder's dogs should have good health clearances. In the United States the Dogo Argentino has a small breed population. The breed only has a small number of dogs currently registered with the Orthopedic Foundation for Animals (OFA). Breeders are currently checking dogs for hip dysplasia.

BAER testing for deafness is also suggested since an estimated 10 percent of dogs can have a pigment-related form of deafness that can affect white dogs (such as Dalmatians, English Setters, and others). BAER-testing (Brainstem Auditory Evoked Response) is a painless test that can be done with puppies when they are as young as five weeks old at a testing centre.

Dogs that are unilaterally or bilaterally deaf should not be used for breeding, if possible. By removing deaf dogs from the breeding pool, the incidence of deafness in the breed will decrease. Note that a unilaterally deaf dog can still make a good pet. Most people will not realize the dog has any particular issues. They simply should not be

Chapter 4: Finding a Dogo Argentino

used for breeding. However, a bilaterally deaf dog often has too many problems to make a safe pet.

Hold every breeder you contact to these standards and this will help narrow down on a breeder for you.

In addition to finding these traits in a breeder, you should also look for the following:

1) Clean facilities

Visit the kennel if you are able to do so, and make sure that it is clean. If you have a breeder that will not let you see the dogs or go to the kennel, choose a different breeder. The only exception to this rule is when the breeder has young puppies in the kennel, that is, less than 4 to 5 weeks of age. At this age some breeders will refuse to allow visitors because disease is easily spread to puppies.

However, if there are no litters, you should be able to go and see the Dogo Argentino puppies. When you get there, check to make sure the home, kennel and grounds are clean. If you notice a lot of dirt, or the dogs are kept in poor conditions, choose a different breeder.

Puppies that come from a dirty, poorly managed kennel can have many health and behavioral problems.

2) Healthy dogs

You can use this same checklist for the adult dogs in the kennel. Often nursing mothers will lose weight and hair, and this is completely normal.

However, the rest of the dogs should look healthy and they should have good energy. It is important not to look at just the parents of the puppies but all the dogs. If any dog looks unwell, question the breeder about it.

Chapter 4: Finding a Dogo Argentino

3) Paperwork

Another important thing to look for is whether there is paperwork. The breeder should have a purchase contract for new puppy owners. In addition, they should have pedigree information, certification and the health clearances for their dogs. They should have registration materials. If they don't, choose a different breeder.

Every good breeder should be utterly committed that none of their dogs end up in rescue. Therefore their contract should have a clause that says the dog has a permanent home with the breeder. It should also have a clause that says the breeder can re-posses the dog if there is significant evidence of abuse or neglect.

4) Puppies raised indoors

While the Dogo Argentino does enjoy time outside, it is important for socialization and health purposes for all puppies to be raised in the home. Puppies raised underfoot will be the most socialized and this will be a benefit to you as the pet owner.

5) Good references

Finally, make sure that the breeder has excellent references. References can come from vets, contacts who have previously bought puppies, and contacts from other breeders.

Remember, when you are choosing your Dogo Argentino breeder, if you come across one that you feel any negative emotions towards, it is recommended that you find another one. Always follow your gut feeling in these cases.

What the breeder expects of you

At the same time, you can expect a breeder to be very suspicious of you, asking you questions, and verifying your references. Dog breeders put a lot of time, effort, and money, not to mention their love for their

Chapter 4: Finding a Dogo Argentino

dogs, into breeding a litter of puppies. It can take years to plan a breeding and produce a litter of puppies. They are often very choosy about who they allow to buy a puppy.

If the breeder gets any negative feelings about you, they have every right to refuse to sell you a puppy. It's not simply a question of going to see the nice puppies and picking out the one you want.

You have to convince the breeder that you will provide a wonderful home for one of their puppies. The breeder may have a questionnaire for you. They may want to visit your home and talk to your veterinary references. Be prepared to talk to the breeder and answer some questions.

There is also some misunderstanding between the general public and dog breeders about how the Internet functions. The general public believes, with some justification, that if you have a web site and show pictures of your dogs and puppies, that you are operating a business and it's okay to ask the price.

Many dog breeders, especially people that breed for dog shows and as a hobby, have web sites so they can show off their dogs. They like to show pictures of their dogs the way proud parents show pictures of their kids. They may have a litter of puppies occasionally but when they get an e-mail from a stranger asking, "How much?" they are both offended and suspicious. They will be likely to think that the person inquiring is planning on doing something terrible to their puppies, like send them to a puppy farm. They will usually ignore that kind of message or send an outraged reply. Yet these are exactly the breeders that do have the best quality puppies.

If you want to contact a show or hobby breeder and enquire about a litter of puppies, it is important to follow the social niceties. Do *not* begin by asking the price. Tell the breeder that you are interested in a puppy. Tell them that you are looking for a pet (if you want a pet). Ask them if they have any puppies. Tell them why you like the dogs. Be candid with the breeder.

Chapter 4: Finding a Dogo Argentino

Experienced breeders can tell when someone is lying to them. Just be honest. But take the time to exchange some messages with the breeder and show a real interest in the puppies instead of bluntly asking the price. Breeders can often work out different kinds of arrangements with someone if they believe the person would provide a good home for one of their puppies. Really loving the breed and the dogs goes a long way.

Adopting an Older Dogo Argentino

Although much of this chapter is focused on finding a Dogo Argentino puppy, it is important to touch on choosing an adult Dogo Argentino. While it is not common, it is possible to find an older Dogo Argentino. This can be a retired dog from a breeding kennel, a rescued dog, or an older puppy that the breeder has decided not to keep.

Adopting an older Dogo Argentino has many advantages:

a) Housebroken: Many adult dogs are housebroken when you adopt them so you don't have to housetrain the dog.

b) Less destructive: This varies from dog to dog but many adult Dogo Argentinos are trained before they go to your home. This means they are less likely to give in to bad habits such as chewing.

c) Affectionate: Although most Dogo Argentinos are affectionate, many older dogs have an almost grateful demeanor with their new owners.

d) Trainable: The old saying, "You can't teach an old dog new tricks", is incorrect because you can teach cues to old dogs. So while many adult Dogo Argentinos will be trained, they can always be taught new cues.

It is important to note that it does take time for an older dog to adjust to their new home and they may be withdrawn during that time. In general, it is recommended that you give the dog about one year to adjust to the change.

Chapter 4: Finding a Dogo Argentino

If you have decided on a Dogo Argentino rescue, contact breeders about older dogs, or Dogo Argentino rescue. We have included some contact information for Dogo Argentino rescue groups in Resources chapter at the back of the book.

Choosing your Dogo Argentino

Once you have selected the breeder and the litter is born, it is time to select the puppy. In most cases the breeder will help determine which puppy is a good match for you. Breeders usually have years of experience and can tell more about a puppy's temperament. They are good at matching puppies with people.

Sometimes a breeder will give you the choice of two or three puppies. Be open about which gender and peculiarities you prefer. It will help the breeder know which puppies might suit you best, although sometimes there may or may not be a choice, depending on the litter. If the litter consists of all males and you have a preference for a female puppy, there's not much the breeder can do about it. You may have to wait for another litter, find a different breeder, or choose a male puppy.

If you are looking for a show puppy, choose one that has the looks and temperament of the breed standard. If you are looking for a pet, you can choose any color and don't have to be so worried about the breed standard. After the selections have been narrowed down between pet and show quality puppies, you can begin your choice. When choosing your puppy, take the time to watch the puppies while they are playing together.

Look for a puppy with an even temperament. Don't believe the myth that the puppy will choose you. Often, the puppy that greets people is the most dominant pup in the litter. While that is not always a bad thing, if you are looking for a quieter puppy, you won't get that with the outgoing puppy.

Instead, look for a puppy that looks around, assesses the situation and then comes to you. This is usually a sign of the middle-of-the-road

Chapter 4: Finding a Dogo Argentino

temperament. Not too reserved where the puppy will be fearful and not too outgoing where they are too pushy.

Don't choose the shy puppy or one that hides. A shy puppy will often grow up to have some temperament problems later in life.

In addition to looking at temperament, look at the health of your puppy. You want to choose a puppy with the following traits:

1) Alert and energetic: Avoid a puppy that seems lethargic. If you arrive during puppy nap time, wait until the Dogo Argentino puppies are awake.

2) Bright eyes: Eyes should be clear of any debris and should not have any discharge. The Dogo Argentino should have dark, lustrous eyes, but they should be alert.

3) Excellent body condition: Look at the overall condition of the body and coat. The coat should be smooth and soft without crusty areas, dandruff, or dullness. The overall body of the puppy should be fat enough where you can't see the ribs but skinny enough that you can feel them when you touch his sides.

4) Nose: Nose should be shiny, black, and wet. In addition, the puppy should have no problems breathing.

5) Excellent sight and hearing: Clap your hands, encourage the puppy to chase toys and watch his reaction. If you see any signs that he can't hear or see, you may want to choose a different puppy.

Although you will be focused on your main choice of puppy, it is important to watch all of the puppies. If you notice signs of disease or sickness in the puppies, choose a different breeder or litter.

It is a very good trait when a puppy doesn't mind being touched and handled. If the puppy struggles or becomes fearful, you may want to discuss a different pick with your breeder.

Chapter 4: Finding a Dogo Argentino

Taking your time and visiting them (more than once if you can) will help you choose the best puppy for you. Remember to use the input of the breeder and be sure to follow your instincts as well.

In the end, this will be a relationship that lasts a very long time, so make sure it is the right one for you and your puppy from the start.

Chapter 5: Getting Ready for your Puppy

Chapter Five: Getting Ready for your Puppy

Getting a puppy is always exciting and part of that excitement comes from preparing for its arrival. While every dog owner is different, there are some common supplies that you should purchase for your Dogo Argentino.

It is important to note that the list of supplies you need for a puppy is pretty basic and you don't need to purchase everything that is recommended by your pet store. In this chapter, we'll look at the supplies that are absolute necessities and supplies that are optional. We will also look at ways for you to "puppy proof" your home.

General Supplies

You don't really need a lot of things when you are getting started with your puppy. However, it is important to have your supplies before you bring your puppy home. For example, you want to have bowls and puppy food ready before you need them. And it's best not to take your puppy shopping with you before he has his vaccinations.

Chapter 5: Getting Ready for your Puppy

Supplies that you should have for your puppy are:

1) Feeding Bowls

Make sure that you have a water and food bowl that your puppy can reach easily. Stainless steel bowls are the best. They are highly durable, they don't break, they are easy to clean, and they don't allow bacteria to grow.

Ceramic bowls are also a good choice, provided they are dishwasher safe. However, if they crack they can allow bacteria to grow. Plastic bowls are not a good choice. Some dogs can be allergic to the plastic and it will cause a reaction on their nose and muzzle. Scratches on the plastic can also harbor bacteria.

2) Harness

Purchase a flat buckle collar for your Dogo Argentino puppy that will fit him when he comes home. Puppies grow quickly so most people purchase a nylon collar for a young puppy instead of purchasing expensive collars that will quickly be outgrown. The general rule is to buy a collar that will allow you to put two fingers between the collar and your puppy's throat. That should be comfortable for your puppy to wear.

3) Leash

A 6-foot flat leash is a good choice for a puppy the size of a Dogo Argentino. You can easily buy a leash that matches your puppy's collar or harness. Remember to use a leash that is comfortable in your hand as well as sturdy. Although you won't need it right away, you may want to purchase a 50-foot (15 meters) lead for teaching the "come" cue later.

You can find feeding bowls, a harness, and leash at your local pet store or check online if you are buying them in advance.

Chapter 5: Getting Ready for your Puppy

4) Dog Grooming Items

Dogo Argentinos don't require a lot of grooming but they do need to be brushed often. While you don't need every type of dog grooming item out there, it is important to have the minimum items for grooming. These include:

a) Undercoat Brush

b) Brush for Long Hair

c) Slicker Brush

d) Nail Clippers

e) Styptic Powder

f) Toothbrush and Toothpaste

g) Dog Shampoo

h) Dog Conditioner

Most pet stores don't have a good selection of grooming tools, but you can find some of these basic implements at the pet store, especially if it's a pet super store. You may need to check online to find some grooming tools. This is especially true if you want to find a good selection of dog shampoos and conditioners.

5) Crate

A crate is a good idea for a Dogo Argentino. While some people don't like them, they are very helpful during housetraining. In addition, it will keep your puppy safe when you can't watch him. Crates are *not* puppy jail. They are a den for dogs and most puppies and dogs enjoy spending time in them. They provide a good place to relax and sleep.

Chapter 5: Getting Ready for your Puppy

When you are choosing a crate for your Dogo Argentino puppy you should keep in mind that your puppy is going to grow. Buy the crate for the size your puppy is going to be as an adult dog. You can easily buy crate "dividers" to make the crate smaller for your puppy. This will keep it the right size while your puppy is growing.

The general rule of thumb is to purchase a crate where the dog can stand up in it and turn around without a problem. It should also have enough room for it to lie down comfortably.

One word of caution with crates is to never crate a dog with his collar on. It is quite easy for the dog's collar to catch on the crate bars and choke the dog.

There are many different kinds of crates. You can choose a hard plastic crate that is used for airline travel. These crates are a good choice if you travel with your dog in your personal vehicle since they provide some protection in case of an accident. Or you can choose a wire crate. These crates are lightweight and easy to fold up and carry. They are a good choice for people who go to shows, obedience trials, and other events. You can also choose a canvas crate – though these are not recommended for dogs that like to use their claws to tear their way out of things.

The puppy should always be trained to use its crate. He must be rewarded for going into the crate, and should never be forced into it.

6) Toys

Toys are not optional for puppies and dogs. They are a necessity. When your puppy begins chewing on something, you can reach for a toy and distract your Dogo Argentino from chewing. If you have ever had a puppy chew your woodwork or furniture, you know that it's much better to spend a little money on toys to entertain your puppy than spend a lot of money repairing your living room.

Chapter 5: Getting Ready for your Puppy

Make sure you choose toys that are recommended for large dogs. Yes, they even make puppy toys for Dogo Argentino puppies. Also, choose puppy toys made for puppies to chew on them. Puppy teeth are sharp and can quickly chew through many toys if they are not made for chewing. The pieces can shred from some toys and bones and can become choking hazards. Choose puppy chew toys that are made with puppy safety in mind.

Pet Safe Busy Buddy toys such as a Tug-a-Jug or a Magic Mushroom are great options.

7) Cleaning Supplies

Cleaning supplies are necessary for bringing a puppy home. Purchase carpet and floor cleaners with enzymes to prevent further soiling.

Also, stock up on paper towels. You will need them.

8) Dog Bed

Finally, purchase a dog bed or a crate bed for your puppy. Even if you allow your puppy up on the furniture, it is good to have something for him to lie on in the crate. A soft faux sheepskin mat is popular with many owners and their dogs. Or, you can use some soft and comfortable blankets. Several cheap towels are best as they are easy to wash. Always assume that anything you give a puppy has a significant chance of being destroyed.

Additional Supplies

In addition to general supplies, there are a few additional supplies that you can purchase for your puppy. Remember, these are optional supplies and you should only buy them if you feel it is necessary.

Chapter 5: Getting Ready for your Puppy

1) Puppy Training Pads

These are pads that you put out for your puppy to potty. They can be used indoors or outdoors. Some people believe they make potty training easier. They are much better than using newspapers if your puppy or dog potties indoors. They have a plastic lining on the bottom to keep liquid from spilling through and a special chemical to encourage your puppy to use them. With a dog the size of a Dogo Argentino you will probably want to train him to potty outside, but puppy training pads can be helpful in the early stages of housetraining.

2) Baby Gates

Baby gates, or pet gates, are a good choice if you want to close off rooms of your house when your puppy comes home. Once your puppy is older and trustworthy in the house (i.e., he won't eat the buttons off your clothes), you can put the baby gates away if you like. Some people use them all the time to keep dogs out of certain parts of the house.

3) Stress Reducing Items

Some people like stress reducing blankets, toys and sprays for puppies, but you probably don't need to spend this money. Instead of purchasing these items, simply take a small doggie blanket to the breeder's home and have them rub it on the mother and siblings of your puppy. This will provide your puppy with the same comfort.

4) Vitamins

While there can be benefits to giving an adult or senior dog vitamins or supplements, you should never do it without the direction of your vet. Some vitamins are toxic when given in high doses so you want to avoid inadvertently poisoning your Dogo Argentino. Giving vitamins and supplements to puppies is **not** advised.

Puppy foods today tend to be very high in fat and Calcium which can be extremely unhealthy for your puppy. We would recommend opting

Chapter 5: Getting Ready for your Puppy

for grain free dog food that is low in calcium (below 0.8%, preferably 0.5%), less than 15% fat, and no more than 25% protein (for slower growth, which is ideal). Anything that is similar to Canidae Grain-Free Pure Land would be a healthy choice. Giving your puppy additional vitamins and minerals can cause musculoskeletal problems later.

When you are choosing your puppy supplies, take your time and start with the essentials, as well as food and treats. After that, anything else is just an added way to spoil your puppy.

Puppy Proofing your Home

Puppy proofing your home is a good way to ensure you and your Dogo Argentino get off to a good start together. Otherwise he could cheerfully destroy your house while he investigates it.

To prevent that destruction, it is important to puppy proof your home before your Dogo Argentino arrives. To properly puppy proof your home, follow the tips below.

1) Put away any hazardous items

Pick up and lock away any items that can be hazardous to your Dogo Argentino. These include:

a) Household cleaning fluids

b) Vitamins

c) Medication

d) Vehicle fluids (such as antifreeze)

e) Salts used to melt ice, or water softeners

f) Pool chemicals

g) Tobacco products

Chapter 5: Getting Ready for your Puppy

2) Puppy's eye view

Take the time to crawl around your home before your puppy arrives and then once or twice a week. Look at things from your puppy's vantage point. Pick up small clips, tags, papers, and anything else that can be a choking hazard for your puppy.

Also, keep clothes picked up. It can be surprising but some articles of clothing, such as socks and underwear, can pose a choking hazard for your Dogo Argentino puppy.

3) Put knick-knacks up high

While you may love having your ornaments on tables and shelves, you would be surprised at what your Dogo Argentino puppy can reach. If he can obtain it, move it up out of reach. Puppies also like to explore by putting things in their mouths. Putting your objects away will prevent the item from being broken and your puppy from getting hurt. It doesn't have to be permanent but only until your Dogo Argentino learns what he is, and is not, allowed to touch.

4) Close off access to standing water

Close toilet seat lids, drain tubs and sinks, and block off any access to a pool if you have one. Standing water can be very tempting for a Dogo Argentino, but can also be a drowning hazard to young puppies, so it is best to be aware of this.

5) Tie up those electrical cords and drapery cords

Electrical cords are always very tempting for a puppy and are often chewed. Always tape your cords out of the reach of your puppy. Also, look for cords that dangle from furniture as the puppy may knock a lamp down on himself while playing with a cord.

Don't forget about computer and phone cords. Make sure they are tucked away, if possible.

Chapter 5: Getting Ready for your Puppy

In addition to electrical cords, pull up the drape or blind cords. These can lead to strangulation if the puppy gets caught in them.

6) Keep garbage out of reach or in a puppy proofed container

Another tempting item for puppies is the garbage can. Always keep it concealed where the puppy is not able to reach it, while ensuring that you empty it every night, especially if he isn't sleeping in its crate.

7) Block off stairs

Even if you allow your Dogo Argentino puppy upstairs with you, block off the stairs at both the top and the bottom. Puppies do not have a lot of coordination and taking stairs can be difficult for them. It is quite common for a puppy to fall down stairs. To prevent this, keep the stairs blocked and off limits.

8) Keep doors closed

Any door or window leading to the outside should be kept closed if the puppy can access it. An open door can be irresistible for a puppy.

9) Check the outdoors

In addition to puppy proofing your house, make sure that you check the outdoors. Look for openings in the fence and items that can be hazardous to your Dogo Argentino puppy. If there are any drainpipes, pools, or other items in your yard, they can present a risk.

The goal is to make the outdoors as safe as the indoors.

10) Look at your plants

Finally, look at the plants that you have in your home and garden. Many plants are poisonous to dogs so avoid having them in your home.

Chapter 5: Getting Ready for your Puppy

If you do have them, make sure they are in areas where your puppy cannot reach them.

In the end, puppy proofing is simply keeping your house neat and tidy – and taking a few precautions. Everyone in the home should work with you to keep the space clean and you should constantly reassess if your house is still safe for your puppy.

Staying on top of puppy proofing will keep your puppy safe.

Toxic Plants

Here is a list of indoor and outdoor plants that you should avoid owning alongside your dog. All of the plants on this list are poisonous in varying degrees to your Dogo Argentino.

Aconite	Emerald Feather	Nightshade
Aloe Vera	English Ivy	Oaks
Amaryllis	Eucalyptus	Oleander
Apple Leaf Croton	European Bittersweet	Onions
Arrow grasses	False Flax	Oriental Lily
Asparagus Fern	False Hellebore	Peace Lily
Atropa belladonna	Fan Weed	Peach Tree
Autumn Crocus	Fiddle-leaf Fig	Pencil Cactus
Azalea	Field Peppergrass	Philodendrons
Baby's Breath	Florida Beauty	Plumosa Fern
Baneberry	Foxglove	Pokeweed
Bird of Paradise	Fruit Salad Plant	Poinsettia
Black Locust	Geranium	Poison Hemlock
Bloodroot	German Ivy	Poison Ivy
Box	Giant Dumb Cane	Poison Oak
Branching Ivy	Glacier Ivy	Potato Plant
Buckeye	Gold Dust Dracaena	Pothos
Buddhist Pine	Golden Pothos	Precatory Bean
Buttercup	Hahn's Self-Branching Ivy	Primrose

The Dogo Argentino Care Guide

Chapter 5: Getting Ready for your Puppy

Caladium	Heartland Philodendron	Rattle box
Calla Lily	Holly	Red Emerald
Carolina Jessamine	Horse Chestnut	Red Princess
Castor Bean	Horse Nettle	Red-Margined Dracaena
Ceriman	Hurricane Plant	Rhododendron
Charming Dieffenbachia	Indian Rubber Plant	Rhubarb
Cherry Tree	Iris	Ribbon Plant
Chinaberry Tree	Jack-in-the-Pulpit	Rosary Pea
Chinese Evergreen	Japanese Show Lily	Saddle Leaf Philodendron
Chock Cherries	Jatropha	Sago Palm
Christmas Berry	Jerusalem Cherry	Satin Pothos
Christmas Rose	Jimsonweed	Schefflera
Cineraria	Kalan Choe	Skunk Cabbage
Clematis	Labarum	Silver Pothos
Common Privet	Lacey Tree Philodendron	Smartweeds
Cordatum	Lantana	Snow-on-the-Mountain
Corn Cockle	Laurels	Sorghum
Corn Plant	Lily of the Valley	Spotted Dumb Cane
Cornstalk Plant	Lupines	Star of Bethlehem
Cowbane	Madagascar Dragon Tree	String of Pearls
Cow Cockle	Manchineel Tree	Striped Dracaena
Cowslip	Marble Queen	Sweetheart Ivy
Croton	Marijuana	Swiss Cheese Plant
Cuban Laurel	Matrimony Vine	Taro Vine
Cutleaf Philodendron	May Apple	Tiger Lily
Cycads	Mexican Breadfruit	Tomato Plant
Cyclamen	Milk Vetch	Tree Philodendron

Chapter 5: Getting Ready for your Puppy

Daffodil	Miniature Croton	Tropic Snow Dieffenbachia
Daphne	Mistletoe	Velvet Grass
Death Camas	Monk's Hood	Weeping Fig
Delphinium	Moonseed	Wild Black Cherry
Devil's Ivy	Morning Glory	Wild Radish
Dieffenbachia,	Mother-in Law's Tongue	Wisteria
Dracaena Palm	Mountain Mahogany	Wood Aster
Dragon Tree	Mustards	Yellow Jessamine
Dumb Cane	Narcissus	Yellow Oleander
Dutchman's Breeches	Needlepoint Ivy	Yellow Pine Flax
Elephant Ears	Nephthytis	Yew

Chapter Six: Bringing your Puppy Home

So you have selected your puppy, purchased the supplies and waited the long weeks before your puppy comes home. This is always an exciting time but it's important to remember that picking your Dogo Argentino puppy up is just as important as caring for him later. That's because your puppy's introduction to your home and family can affect his development and the bond you develop later.

In this chapter, we'll go over everything you need to know about bringing your Dogo Argentino puppy home.

Chapter 6: Bringing your Puppy Home

The Day of Pick Up

The day you pick up your Dogo Argentino puppy is always exciting. If you haven't been lucky enough to find a breeder with puppies, it can mean that you have waited months or even years to source your puppy. It can be difficult to stay calm but it is important to do so for the sake of your puppy. Puppies are often nervous and scared during this time of transition. When you are calm, it is reassuring to your puppy.

You can begin taking steps to make the transition go smoothly before you even arrive at the breeder's house. If possible, send a blanket to the breeder a few days ahead of time and ask her to rub it on your puppy's siblings and mother. If it isn't possible, bring the blanket with you when you pick him up. Your puppy can start to become accustomed to your scent and associate it with the comforting smells of his current family.

In some cases you may be picking up a puppy at the airport, especially. If you have found a breeder that lives a long distance from you. If this is the case, then you and the breeder should discuss everything over the phone ahead of time. The breeder should have the puppy's vaccination records and health certificate, as well as his other travel papers so he can fly. Airlines have on occasional instances killed animals in cargo. For an 8 – 12 month old puppy it will certainly be a traumatic experience that will be with them for a long time, so bear this in mind.

Some countries require quarantine procedures when a dog enters the country. Be sure to find out if your country requires any kind of quarantine when dogs are imported.

You will need to make sure that you have all of the puppy's travel information from the breeder so you know where and when the puppy is arriving. Different airlines handle shipping dogs in different ways, so it's a good idea to call the airline ahead of time and make sure you have the details correct. Cargo offices are not always open 24 hours a day, so make sure you will be able to pick up your puppy right after the plane arrives.

Chapter 6: Bringing your Puppy Home

Resist the temptation to open your puppy's crate door as soon as you see him at the airport. Dogs can and do get lost at airports. Wait until you have the crate safely secured in your vehicle before you open the door. Once you have your puppy's collar (or harness) and leash on, you can stop at a rest area and let him potty and give him some fresh water.

It's usually best if you leave your children at home when you pick up your new Dogo Argentino puppy. This is true whether you are picking the puppy up at the breeder's home or going to the airport. It's a good idea to discuss your children with the breeder so they can help you choose which puppy is best-suited to live with kids. This is important because bringing your puppy home can be a stressful time for your Dogo Argentino and the excitement of children can make it more so. Before you leave to collect the puppy, have everything set up for him so you can simply bring him home and take him to his safe place.

If you are picking your puppy up at the breeder's house, place a crate in your car for your Dogo Argentino to travel home in. Puppies should never sit in the driver's lap or be loose in the car. It is much too easy for a puppy to distract the driver and cause an accident.

Once you arrive at the breeder's house, spend some time with your puppy, his litter-mates, his mother, and with the breeder. If you have some last minute questions, try to have them written down so you won't forget them. Building a good relationship with your puppy's breeder is important. They will be a valuable resource for you throughout your puppy's life.

After you leave the breeder's home, you should go straight home. Don't stop to visit a friend or go to a pet store. Every place you stop can expose your Dogo Argentino puppy to disease at this age and to extra stress. Try to keep your puppy calm and don't worry. Your puppy will soon be able to visit friends and go places with you.

Keep an eye on your Dogo Argentino puppy in the car. Many puppies experience motion sickness in cars. It's possible that your puppy has already taken some car trips to the vet, but some puppies will still get

Chapter 6: Bringing your Puppy Home

car sick. If you see your puppy's nose drooping towards the floor, or drooling and wrinkling his lips, pull over and allow him time to get over his car sickness. He may throw up but that is perfectly normal. It's a good idea to take some paper towels and cleaner with you. This is another reason why we recommend crating your puppy on the ride home. It's easier to clean the crate if your puppy becomes sick, in comparison to having to clean your entire car.

If you do have to stop, whether for a potty break or because your puppy is car sick, try to stop at secluded spots where you won't see a lot of dogs. Take him to an area to potty and then immediately pick him up. Avoid other dogs as you don't know which ones have been properly vaccinated.

When you arrive home, immediately take your puppy outside to potty. Puppies will usually sniff around the yard and then relieve themselves. Once your puppy has relieved himself, you can enter the house and go to a quiet room together.

Sit with your Dogo Argentino puppy and allow him the opportunity to explore his surroundings. Some Dogo Argentino puppies will want to play and run around, others will want to sleep. Follow your puppy's cues.

You can introduce your puppy slowly to family members. Keep all interactions with the new puppy calm. During the first few days you will find your Dogo Argentino sleeps a lot. This is normal for all puppies at a young age. However, this will change as he becomes familiar with his home and as he gets older and gains confidence.

As far as house rules are concerned, you should start the way you mean to continue. Keep to a schedule for housetraining and stick to the rules. A schedule will help your puppy know when and where he is supposed to potty. If your Dogo Argentino will not be allowed to sleep on your bed when he's an adult dog, don't let him up when he is a cute puppy.

Chapter 6: Bringing your Puppy Home

Keep your puppy confined to one area and then slowly open up your home to your puppy as he becomes more confident and trustworthy. In reality, the key to introducing your puppy to his new home is being calm, progressing slowly, and creating rules and schedules.

Introducing your Dogo Argentino to other family members

Once your puppy is home, it's time to introduce him to the other residents in your home. While your first instinct is probably to rush in and introduce him to everyone, your puppy can become very frightened or overwhelmed by too much attention all at once. A puppy can withdraw and shut down if he is overwhelmed by his surroundings or by meeting too many people.

Since you want all introductions to be positive, it's best to make the introductions as calmly as possible. Let your puppy have time to get used to his new home.

One of the best things that you can do for your puppy when you bring him home is to allow him to rest in a quiet room. After he has had some time to adjust, start bringing in people to meet him, one at a time.

Other animals in the home can wait a day or two. There is no rush and you want to do the introductions properly to prevent any lasting problems for your Dogo Argentino.

Children

For younger children, it's a good idea to introduce them to your Dogo Argentino puppy one at a time. This will help minimize the amount of stimulation the puppy has. If you have older children, you can introduce them together.

When you are introducing your Dogo Argentino puppy to children, start by having your child come into the room and sit down on the floor. Don't rush the puppy or place the puppy in your child's lap.

Chapter 6: Bringing your Puppy Home

Instead, give the child treats to feed the puppy and allow the puppy to approach on his own terms. Tell the child to stay calm and quiet so the puppy won't get frightened.

Dogo Argentinos have a natural fondness for children so your puppy should gravitate to the child. When the puppy does greet the child, let the child pet the Dogo Argentino calmly.

Keep meetings short and build up their length. In addition, over the first few days, make all interactions with the children calm and quiet. As the puppy gets used to the sounds of children, you can start introducing play times.

It's important that children should have rules regarding the puppy and they should be taught how to treat it. Make sure your children understand the following rules:

a) Be calm around the puppy.

b) Don't hold onto him when he wants to go.

c) Never hit or pinch the puppy.

d) Don't pull on ears or tail.

e) Gently pet the puppy.

f) Use toys to play with the puppy.

g) Don't try to take toys or food away from a puppy or dog.

h) Don't run away from a puppy or dog.

Unfortunately, most puppies and dogs don't respect children the same way they do the adult (taller) members of the family. Your children won't be able to command your puppy with the same authority that you have until they are a little older. It's important that an adult is always present to supervise when small children play with puppies and dogs to

Chapter 6: Bringing your Puppy Home

keep accidents from happening. Once your children are a little older, your dog will respect them more and play is less likely to get out of hand.

As you train your Dogo Argentino puppy, you should include your children in the puppy's training and socialization. This will be helpful for both your puppy and your children in the long run.

The Dogo Argentino has been specifically bred to be a good dog at home with children. However, it is still your responsibility to teach both your puppy and your children how to interact with each other. Supervise their play, especially with small children, to avoid any problems.

Other Pets

When deciding on a puppy, it's a good idea to take into account your current pets, especially if you already have a dog. The Dogo Argentino usually does best in a home with another dog of the opposite sex. Otherwise, you may have skirmishes between two males or two females later as they try to be top dog in the home.

Introducing your Dogo Argentino puppy to other pets in the home is something that you should do gradually. Remember that the animals in the home were there first and they can have some behavioral problems with a new puppy such as jealousy or problems with territory.

To prevent these problems, make sure that you make the meetings short. Also ensure that you do not force any relationships. The animals in your home will sort out their hierarchy on their own.

When introducing other pets, it is important to follow these rules:

1) Keep your puppy confined

The first rule is that you should always keep your puppy confined when you bring him home. Place your Dogo Argentino in a quiet room. This

Chapter 6: Bringing your Puppy Home

will keep your puppy safe while still making your current pet feel confident.

When you are bringing the puppy out of his room, confine the current dog unless you are taking the time to introduce them.

2) Allow door sniffing

You can allow door or crate sniffing. What this means is that you should allow your current pet to sniff at the crate or the door where the puppy is. Don't let them be pushy and if your puppy starts to look stressed, stop the behavior.

Sniffing at the door will help your pet become acquainted with the puppy while there is a safe barrier between the pet and the puppy.

3) Set up the meeting

Plan meetings in advance, between your current pet, and your puppy. Never bring in a puppy and then allow your current pet to take charge. Instead, wait until your current pet is calm before you make the introductions. This will help promote a positive experience for both your new Dogo Argentino and your current pet.

4) Encourage your current pet to accept your puppy with positivity

When you are doing the introductions, always provide your current pet with plenty of affection. Give him lots of praise for greeting nicely and make sure that you give him plenty of treats. The more you praise your current pet, the more he will think the new Dogo Argentino puppy is something positive.

5) Let cats greet on their own terms

While you can control the meetings between a dog and puppy, it can be difficult to control the meeting between a puppy and cat. Often, puppies find cats interesting (too interesting) and will try to chase the cat or play with him. When this happens, the cat will usually react.

Chapter 6: Bringing your Puppy Home

The best thing to do is to allow the cat to watch the Dogo Argentino puppy from his own vantage points. Praise, treat, and pet the cat when you are able so he will be comfortable with the new excitement in the home.

After a few weeks, start bringing your cat down from his perches, but only when the puppy is calm. Do not introduce the cat in the middle of a play session. Always make sure that you have control of your Dogo Argentino puppy to prevent him from chasing the cat.

It may take time but eventually your Dogo Argentino will come to make friends with the cat, though it will always be on the cat's terms.

6) Make the older pet the primary pet

What this means is that your current pet should have more rights than the puppy. The current pet should be fed first, you should greet him first when you arrive home, and you should always allow the current pet to enter or exit first.

It may be hard to believe, but if you support your older pet's position, it shows the puppy that he must respect the older pet. You will avoid fights over status and rank if you back your older pet's rights. Your puppy may try to challenge your older pet's authority from time to time, but it's up to you to support your older pet if you want peace in your home, unless the puppy has been rewarded and should be allowed to keep his reward, such as a marrow bone.

Rewards should always be merit based. A good rule is to watch them carefully and we contention occurs, then separate and reward both for the separation. This will teach them that they will be rewarded for simply disengaging.

As the animals become more acquainted, you can start offering more attention and other things equally but for the first few months, make the current pet feel extra special.

Chapter 6: Bringing your Puppy Home

7) Be patient

Finally, be patient with your pets. Remember that this is a big adjustment for them and that they may not warm up quickly. In fact, many times it can take up to 6 months for the puppy to be accepted by the current pets. For cats, it can take up to a year.

Socialization and the First Few Weeks

We'll discuss socialization for your Dogo Argentino puppy more thoroughly a little later, but we should touch on it here. Socialization is an important aspect of your puppy's life and it actually starts from the moment he is born.

Before he even comes home with you, your breeder has probably already begun socializing your puppy. Puppies that are raised in a home environment learn about vacuums, televisions, music, meeting people, and receive much affection and petting from the moment they are born. Most breeders will take puppies outside to let them experience the grass and other surfaces. Puppies usually go to the vet and meet some friendly strangers there. In addition, your Dogo Argentino puppy's mother and litter-mates will also teach him puppy manners so he has some idea of how to behave with other dogs.

However, after you bring your puppy home, it is up to you to continue to socialize your Dogo Argentino. Many trainers will recommend puppy classes after 16 weeks of age and won't stress socialization until after those classes start. Puppy kindergarten classes are important and they are recommended for the Dogo Argentino, but you should be socializing your puppy well before 16 weeks. The crucial time period for puppy socialization is between 7 to 12 weeks of age.

Obviously, between 3 and 8 weeks of age, your puppy will be socialized at the breeder's home. However, between 8 to 16 weeks, you need to take the time to work on socialization. The reason why this is a crucial period is because during this time, puppies are less fearful and more open to new experiences.

Chapter 6: Bringing your Puppy Home

Between 7 and 9 weeks of age, the Dogo Argentino puppy will start to become more cautious around new objects and subjects. This can make socialization harder. The main problem with this window is the fact that your Dogo Argentino cannot go to many places until he has had his second set of vaccinations. However, you can still work on socialization at home.

During the first few weeks at home, from 8 to 16 weeks, take the time to socialize your puppy to a range of different stimuli in the house. For example, continue to expose your puppy to the same things he probably experienced at the breeder's home: vacuum, watch television, and have guests over.

Make sure that you touch your puppy and handle him often so he can become socialized to your touch. After your puppy is 10 weeks old, or has had his second set of shots, take your puppy to places where puppies and dogs are welcome and continue his socialization with others.

Puppies will continue to go through different stages as they grow and develop, including more fear stages.

The Critical Fear Periods in Puppies

a) Seven to Nine Weeks

b) Four to Six Months

c) Approximately Eight to Nine Months

d) Approximately Twelve Months

e) Approximately Fourteen to Eighteen Months

During these stages your puppy can be fearful of people, places, and objects that he already knows. He might bark at very ordinary things. He might shake or hide from something that wouldn't normally bother him. This is all normal behavior for your puppy during these stages.

Chapter 6: Bringing your Puppy Home

Stick to familiar routines during these times. Reward positive behavior and try not to encourage fearful behavior.

As a rule you should expose your puppy to anything that it will be expected to deal with as an adult. You must anticipate some fear responses, so take valuable treats with you and be prepared to counter-condition in case of any fear responses.

For more information on socialization, read Chapter Eight, on socializing your Dogo Argentino.

Chapter Seven: Caring for your Dogo Argentino

Caring for your Dogo Argentino does not have to be something that is overly complicated. Despite the fact that they are a large, powerful dog, they are normally easy to care for.

In this chapter, we'll go over everything you need to know about taking care of your Dogo Argentino, on a day-to-day basis.

Grooming

The Dogo Argentino has a short, smooth coat that sheds regularly. They don't require a lot of grooming but they do need to be brushed often (at least 2 times per week) to help remove the dead coat. You may need to brush a little more often when your dog is shedding.

You can expect to brush your Dogo Argentino a couple of times per week and bathe as necessary. You can use a rubber curry comb to

Chapter 7: Caring for your Dogo Argentino

loosen and remove some of the dead hair. Curry combs are also available from pet stores and online from pet product retailers.

You will also need to keep your dog's nails trimmed. If this is something you are uncomfortable doing yourself, veterinarians will often cut nails for their clients or you can visit a pet groomer.

You will also need to check your dog's ears regularly to make sure they are clean. We also recommend that you brush your dog's teeth often. You can purchase a doggy toothbrush and doggy toothpaste at a pet store or online. Do not use human toothpaste. It can contain xylitol (an artificial sweetener) which is toxic to dogs. Doggy toothpaste comes in flavors dogs such as peanut butter and beef. Most dogs enjoy having their teeth brushed and think the toothpaste is a treat.

Although many people view grooming as a chore, it can actually be a very pleasant activity for you and your Dogo Argentino. It provides you with an opportunity to bond with your dog and also creates a period of quiet time for your Dogo Argentino.

In addition, it helps you stay on top of health problems with your dog since part of grooming is checking over their health. You can check your dog's body for any lumps or bumps that might be a cause of concern. Grooming your dog also gives you a chance to check and treat for fleas and ticks.

It's a good idea to groom puppies daily. There isn't a lot of real grooming to do, but it's a great way to get your puppy used to being touched and handled. Take the time to touch his paws, tail, head and body. Make it a positive experience with treats and praise. If you start off in this way with your puppy, grooming will always be easy and enjoyable for both of you.

Bathing

Bathing is not something that needs to be done frequently with a Dogo Argentino. They don't usually get very dirty nor do they have a strong

Chapter 7: Caring for your Dogo Argentino

dog odor. Too much bathing can dry out the skin, removing the coat's natural oils, which will damage the coat and cause you more problems.

Bathing once every month or two is usually more than enough to keep your Dogo Argentino clean. Before bathing, you should brush your Dogo Argentino with a slicker brush to remove any dead hair. When bathing, use a gentle, cleansing coat shampoo for dogs. Avoid human shampoos as the many chemicals and additives to human shampoo often dry out a dog's coat. You can also use a dog coat conditioner after bathing if you wish.

Bathe your Dogo Argentino in warm water and make sure that you always rinse the coat completely. Leaving shampoo residue can lead to dandruff or irritation of the skin.

Nail Clipping

Clipping your dog's nails is another important part of regular care. Nail clipping, and the frequency of clipping, differs from dog to dog. Some dogs require their nails to be clipped once a week, others once a month. Where you live, the flooring and ground outside, and other factors, as well as the individual dog, will determine how long the nails grow and how often they need to be trimmed.

To properly clip your Dogo Argentino's nails, you can either use a traditional clipper, which has a sharp blade or a dremel tool. Dremels, which are small sanding tools, keep the nail smooth. If the quick is cut, which is the vein in each nail, the dremel tool will cauterize the cut and prevent bleeding. However, some dogs object to the noise the dremel makes. If you plan to use a dremel on your dog's nails, it helps to begin when your dog is a puppy.

Nail clippers are easy to use but you run the risk of cutting the nail too short, which can be painful to your dog. If you cut your dog's nails too short once or twice, your dog can become foot shy and clipping his nails becomes a struggle.

Chapter 7: Caring for your Dogo Argentino

When you are clipping your dog's nails, hold the paw firmly in one hand. Holding the tool at a 90 degree angle with the nail, grind or make a small cut. Never take a lot of nail off at one time. Instead, make small cuts and slowly work your way back. It's much better to trim a small amount and shorten the nails over the course of several days or weeks than try to make them too short in one session.

In dogs with black nails you won't be able to see the quick from the outside of the nail. You will need to simply cut back until you start to see a grey oval inside the nail. This is the main indication that you are close to the quick.

If you happen to cut the quick you can stop the bleeding by dipping the nail in cornstarch or styptic powder. Although your dog will yelp in pain, it is important to cut another nail on the dog before you end the session. The reason for this is so the dog does not end a nail clipping session on a negative. End every grooming session with a positive so your Dogo Argentino realizes that grooming is a positive thing.

We recommend giving your dog a treat and lots of praise as you trim every nail. Let your dog know that getting his nails done is something good. Be lavish with your treats and praise.

Brushing

Brushing your Dogo Argentino has many benefits:

a) Allows you to bond with your dog.

b) Helps distribute natural oils through your dog's coat.

c) Removes dead skin.

d) Removes dead hair.

e) Allows you an opportunity to check the health of your dog's body.

Chapter 7: Caring for your Dogo Argentino

When your Dogo Argentino is young, it is important to spend time simply brushing and petting him during a grooming session. This will make grooming very positive for your Dogo Argentino and will ensure that he enjoys it. It will also give you the opportunity to look over your dog and make sure that he is healthy and happy.

To brush a Dogo Argentino you can use a good bristle brush, such as the boar bristle brush. Brush your dog going in the direction of hair growth, not against it.

Brushing should only take 5 to 10 minutes. End every brushing session with a treat so your dog will look forward to being groomed.

Ears

In most countries the Dogo Argentino has cropped ears to prevent prey animals from grabbing and biting them. If the ears were left long they could be caught and torn easily. If you hunt with your dog – or even if you don't – you should check your dog's ears carefully, inside and out, to make sure they are clean and healthy.

If your dog has any kind of ear infection, you can expect to find a strong odor coming from the ears. Finding mud or other dirt on the inner ear flap is not a sign that your dog has an ear problem. Ear infections occur in the ear canal.

To clean the ears you should never stick anything inside the ear canal. For example, q-tips will often push the debris down into the ear and this will cause more problems.

You can buy ear cleaning solution for dogs from your veterinarian or at the pet store. Soak a cotton ball in the solution. Place the swab into the ear and then massage the base of the ear. Remove the swab and wipe the outside of the ear canal and the overall ear until they are clean. You can repeat this process as long as any debris or wax continues to come up from the ear canal.

Chapter 7: Caring for your Dogo Argentino

Check the inside of the ears for any hair and trim or pull it if there is hair growing down inside the ear canal. Keeping the ear clear of too much hair allows air to flow to the ear and discourages bacteria from growing. It's a good way to prevent ear infections.

Remember to never put anything down into the ears that is smaller than your finger and if you see any type of unusual discharge, take your dog to the vet.

Teeth

The final thing you should attend to for your Dogo Argentino is his teeth. Unlike people, dogs do not need their teeth brushed several times a day. Instead, you can brush them several times a week.

When you brush your dog's teeth, make sure that you use a canine toothbrush. If you haven't introduced your dog to brushing, start with just the toothbrush without toothpaste.

Never use human toothpaste as it can make a dog sick. Use toothpaste that is made for dogs instead. You can buy toothbrushes and toothpaste made for dogs at a pet store or online. Most dogs like having their teeth brushed once they are introduced to it.

When brushing the teeth, all you need to brush are the outside surface of the teeth.

If you don't like the idea of brushing your Dogo Argentino's teeth, some people use a spray or add a liquid to their dog's drinking water that will help keep the teeth cleaner. The chemical ingredient is chlorhexidine gluconate. It's an antiseptic/antibacterial disinfectant oral rinse. It's often found in mouthwashes. If you wish to use it for your dog, be sure to buy a version made for dogs.

Alternatively, many owners have had much success with feeding their Dogo Argentino Sweet Potato dog chews. They are practical, time saving, and in some cases will do a better job than the owner equipped with a tooth brush and paste.

Chapter 8: Socializing your Dogo Argentino

Chapter Eight: Socializing your Dogo Argentino

One important aspect of owning a Dogo Argentino is to properly socialize it. While many people think of socializing as something you do when your Dogo Argentino is a puppy, it is actually important to do it throughout the life of your dog.

Even a perfectly socialized dog can slip into bad habits from time to time. If you continue to socialize regularly, you can keep this from happening.

In this chapter we'll go over the key points of socializing your Dogo Argentino.

Chapter 8: Socializing your Dogo Argentino

Socializing your Dogo Argentino

Socializing your Dogo Argentino is an important step in developing a well rounded dog. In many ways, socialization begins the moment the puppies are born. There are many things that your breeder will do that will establish good socialization patterns with the puppies.

Generally, when we think of socialization, we think of it in terms of being social with others. This can be with people, other dogs, or children. While being "social" is one important aspect of socializing, it is just that, one aspect.

Instead of focusing socialization on one area, it's important to focus on socializing the complete dog. Socialize the dog to a range of stimuli and this will help create a sound dog that doesn't frighten easily. The whole point of socialization is to build self-confidence in your dog so he can calmly interact with the human world. Let's look at ways to build that confidence.

What is Socialization?

Socialization means to be part of society. What this means when we apply it to dogs is that a dog needs to be a productive part of their human surroundings. They should be taught to accept things they will see on a day-to-day basis. In addition, they should accept people and other animals.

Socialization is when we expose a puppy and/or dog to a host of different stimuli and encourage them to accept or not even notice that stimuli.

The process of socialization is very important since dogs that are not properly socialized can become timid and fearful. In addition, they can become aggressive to animals, other dogs, and to people.

Chapter 8: Socializing your Dogo Argentino

When Should I Socialize?

Socialization is a lifelong process. However, socialization should begin as soon as possible. Every day counts in this. You just need to be careful about disease prevention when socializing a young puppy.

The key period of socialization is between the ages of 6 weeks to 5 months old. During that time, your Dogo Argentino will go through various developmental milestones, which will go smoothly if socialization is done properly.

In addition to these periods, you should be aware that puppies will go through fear periods. Your confident Dogo Argentino may suddenly become a very fearful little puppy almost overnight. This is normal and you simply continue socializing your puppy as you normally would.

Fear periods in dogs differ depending on the breed but you should expect this to be between 5 to 7 months of age and then, possibly, again around 16 to 18 months of age.

How do I socialize?

Socialization is done in small amounts and it is important to follow a few rules to help keep socialization positive. Remember that you want your Dogo Argentino to accept things as a positive and not to be afraid. If something is negative, then the dog will have more problems than if he wasn't socialized at all.

Chapter 8: Socializing your Dogo Argentino

Make the Socialization Fun

Always make sure that every socialization time that he has is a fun one. Let the puppy play around the stimuli so that he can learn that it is not a negative thing.

Let It Be at His Pace

Although our first response is to nudge our puppy closer to the thing we are socializing him to, it is important to allow your Dogo Argentino to approach the object at his own pace.

It may take several socialization experiences before the puppy will go and approach the new item but you should take your time. Never force the experience or push the dog towards the stimuli.

Give your Dogo Argentino Space

Sit close to your Dogo Argentino so you can be a reassurance to him but also let him have space. You want him to feel like he can retreat and approach the stimuli as he likes. If he feels cornered or trapped, it will make the socialization a negative experience.

When it comes to people, use the same rule. Have them sit away from the puppy and then allow the puppy to go and greet them.

Mix it up

Another important rule is to mix up the socialization. Your Dogo Argentino may have no problem interacting with dogs when he is in his home but outside of his home may be a different story. Take the time to set up socialization outside of the house and in the house. Take him to a variety of places, and introduce him to the same things you introduced in the home, within reason. For example, you are not as likely to run into a vacuum on the street.

Do the reverse when he is at home. Often, people forget the importance of inviting others over so the Dogo Argentino can learn to accept things

Chapter 8: Socializing your Dogo Argentino

both in his house and outside of it. It will also help if you make visitors an accepted norm.

Use Reinforcement

Finally, use rewards for reinforcement when you are socializing your puppy. Things like treats, verbal encouragement, and praise will help your Dogo Argentino be successful with a socialization exercise.

Never force your puppy to be brave. If they wish to retreat to what they feel is a safer distance. Let them do so, even encourage this. (Contrary to popular myth, it is impossible to reinforce fear, as Dr. Suzanne Hetts, Dr. Daniel Q. Estep and Suzanne Clothier have conclusively proven.)

After they have withdrawn to a safer distance, let them approach again and if they want to leave again, let them do so. Keep repeating that while rewarding approaching whatever it is they are unsure of. If your puppy shows any fear or reactivity, the B.A.T. Protocol, by Grisha Stewart, may be able to help you overcome this challenge.

What Should I Socialize To?

You may be wondering what you should use for socializing your puppy. While everyone has different living circumstances that will change your socialization stimuli, there are a number of stimuli that you should use for your puppy no matter where you live. Below is a checklist to get you started with socializing your Dogo Argentino:

Stimuli	X	Stimuli	X
Men: Bearded and clean-shaven		Balls of various size	
Women		Mirrors	
Children: Boys and Girls		Baby strollers	
Toddlers: Boys and Girls		Grocery carts	

66   The Dogo Argentino Care Guide

Chapter 8: Socializing your Dogo Argentino

Babies: Boys and Girls		Mirrors	
People with glasses		Brooms	
People with crutches		Dusters	
People with canes		Vacuum cleaners	
People in wheelchairs		Wind	
Slouched people		Flags	
People with walkers		Tents	
Shuffling people		Flashlights	
Large crowds		Children's Toys	
Small crowds		Television	
People on roller blades		Plastic bags	
People of various shapes and sizes: tall, thin, heavy, short, etc.		Umbrellas	
People with sunglasses		Balloons	
People who are exercising		Skateboards	
People on bikes		Children playing	
Costumes		Hammering	
Bald people		Construction equipment	
Big dogs		Lawn mowers	
Little dogs		Scooters	
Farm animals		Buses	
Puppies		Trains	
Small Rodent/non canine		Sirens	
Birds		Ceiling fans	
Lizards		Garage doors	

The Dogo Argentino Care Guide

Chapter 8: Socializing your Dogo Argentino

Escalators	Dremel tools
Cars: Both while walking and riding in them	Fireworks
Sliding doors	Cheering
Planes (optional)	Yelling
Elevators	Radios
Escalators	Storms
Alarms	Loud noises
Singing	Visiting the vet
Grooming	Getting nails cut
Being crated	Being picked up
Having all body parts touched	Leash
Collar	Harnesses

As you can see, there is a lot to socialize your Dogo Argentino to and this table only touches on some of the more common stimuli.

Classes

Classes are another good way to socialize your Dogo Argentino. Puppy kindergarten classes and puppy pre-school classes are an excellent way to let your Dogo Argentino puppy interact with other puppies and people. This provides wonderful opportunities for socialization in a controlled environment.

Your puppy can also learn a few obedience basics at the same time. Most of these classes are offered through local kennel clubs, training centers, or specific pet stores. They usually offer the opportunity for puppies to enter a basic obedience class late.

Chapter Nine: Training your Dogo Argentino

We will cover training your Dogo Argentino in this chapter. However, it does not replace the advice and training of a Certified Professional Dog Trainer. If your means allow for it, we strongly suggest you enroll your Dogo Argentino puppy in puppy kindergarten or puppy pre-school classes. We encourage you to follow up with a good basic obedience class when your puppy is a little older. This will also offer ample socialization to your puppy.

Also, should you wish to use one, please do research when hiring a trainer. Not all dog trainers are created equal. Ask about continuing education and any certifications they may have, and what they must do to keep them current. Dog training is a totally unregulated field and anyone at all can call themselves a dog trainer and not be accountable to anyone. There had even been a case of a pet dying from abuse resulting from poor "training" in New Jersey, U.S.

So it is best to seek out a trainer who is certified by an independent certifying body that is not monetarily motivated by any manufacturers

Chapter 9: Training your Dogo Argentino

of training equipment or food. Two fine examples are CCPDT (the Certification Council for Professional Dog Trainers) or IAABC (International Association of Animal Behavior Consultants).

Training Basics

It is important to actively work to engage your Dogo Argentino in a way that is both fulfilling and understandable to him or he will quickly lose interest and find something else to do. This is best achieved with the use of a clicker or the word 'Yes!' as a marker of good performance.

Always use a marker to inform the dog that he has performed correctly. You must pair the marker word or the click with the treats by repeatedly clicking or saying the marker word as you deposit treats in the dog's mouth. Through this technique, the dog will learn that the click or the marker word means a treat.

This is necessary in order to communicate to the dog that he has done something correct at the occurrence of the desired behavior. Remember, dogs only have a memory of their own behavior for approximately half a second after the behavior has occurred.

Therefore, it is essential that we have a way to communicate good performance on the instant that it happens in order for the dog to understand that it has done something well. This is why it is best to use a clicker or a marker word to achieve this rather than trying to deliver a treat within half a second of the correct behavior. One would have to be a veritable ninja with treats to make this work without the marker!

You can then apply the clicker or the marker word to teaching your Dogo Argentino any type of behavior, such as a collar grab. To do this, every time you reach down and touch the collar, click or say the marker word and give your dog a treat.

The reason for the latter is to let your dog know that touching the collar is not bad. Often, when we give a cue, such as 'come', 'sit' or 'heel', it

Chapter 9: Training your Dogo Argentino

is because we want to gain control of them. If we don't train a dog to become familiar with having their leash touched, the dog may get into the habit of running from you when you go to grab his collar.

Molly Sumner, A Certified Professional Dog Trainer (Certified Canine Behavior Consultant and Certified Behavioral Adjustment Training Instructor), from New Jersey, U.S. has some useful insights about training.

When asked what the key to training this breed is, she had this to say:

"I think there are a few elements that are more important than any others. First, you need a clicker. It's a very distinctive sound that when paired effectively with the right food reward, serves as the best communication tool available. You also need to understand that reinforcement is a far larger category than just food. You need the patience of a saint and you need to be 100% committed to getting what you want. Maybe not today, maybe not tomorrow, maybe not next week, but eventually. However long that might be. You need the animal to trust you completely, not just to give rewards, but to step in and remove things that are making it uncomfortable or remove the animal if it becomes too agitated. Feeling safe and secure is extremely important for a primitive breed." - Molly Sumner.

Taking that excerpt piece by piece, we will discuss the clicker or the "Yes!" marker first.

1) Have a great deal of treats in your treat pouch or in a bowl out of the dog's reach.

2) Click the clicker and/or say the "Yes!" marker at the same time as you deposit a treat in the dog's mouth.

3) Repeat this continuously, as fast as you can for about 5 to 10 minutes a day for the first week and then once a week thereafter to maintain the association.

Chapter 9: Training your Dogo Argentino

If you do this consistently, you will have trained a very effective reward marker and your dog will think the clicker or the word "Yes!" is the best thing ever and a motivating sound in its own right.

What she means by patience is that training doesn't happen in a day or even a week or a month. If the dog just isn't grasping "Down", keep trying. If you still can't get it, do something the dog does know, reward for that, and come back to "Down" later. By staying "100% committed to getting what you want." She means that these dogs learn more from us than we think. If, in the end, not the beginning, you settle for less than what you want; the dog will learn that it doesn't actually have to perform correctly at all.

Remember, if you miss that half-second window immediately after the desired behavior has been performed, the dog will be confused as to why it earned the treat. There also must be a relationship of trust between you. The dog needs to be secure in the knowledge that you will not place him in an uncomfortable situation and just expect him to "deal with it." You must make every effort to manage his state of mind if you want the best results.

Before you start training your puppy or dog, ensure that you accept that this process may take some time. You should adjust your expectations and be happy with small degrees of progress. They are smart dogs and they can learn quickly. Whether they choose to obey you is another matter. This is where your relationship and trust with your Dogo Argentino become important. If your dog can trust you completely to pay him for his work, and make it fun, then you will have little trouble motivating him.

With that said, do not imagine for one moment that you can bully this breed into compliance. Dogo Argentinos expect to be companions and partners. The best policy is calm insistence on what you want and never giving up on it. Even if it means revisiting it in order to achieve the desired result.

Chapter 9: Training your Dogo Argentino

Rules

The Dogo Argentino does require rules and it is of dire importance that you be consistent with them. Before you bring your puppy home, think of the rules that you want to have in your house. If you are fine with dogs on the furniture, allow it. If not, don't allow it from the very moment your puppy comes home. It may not seem like a big deal but it will confuse your Dogo Argentino when you finally tell him to stay off.

When you are training your Dogo Argentino, be sure to follow these rules:

1. Manners

Always insist on manners. Never under any circumstances allow a puppy to practice behaviors that you would find undesirable in an adult dog. This means that jumping up should never be practiced. If the puppy does jump up, even once, turn your back on him and make like a tree.

Removing your attention from a puppy is a more effective discourager than anything else. If the puppy still continues to jump, confine them to another area and try again in a few minutes. The rule is that the puppy may not get away with poor manners. This is a good time to ask for a sit and reward instead of jumping. Remember, give the puppy something it can get right.

2. Make him Work

Regardless of whether you are giving him food, a treat or praise, you want your dog to work for it. Always give your Dogo Argentino a cue, such as "sit" and "wait" at dinner-time, before you give him some form of reward. This will teach him that he needs to work for things and will also help with manners so he is not jumping or grabbing at things.

The Dogo Argentino Care Guide

Chapter 9: Training your Dogo Argentino

3. Be the Initiator

Playing, cuddling, and any type of attention should be done with you initiating it. Pick up toys, although you can leave out a few to combat chewing, and bring them out for play sessions.

Do not give in if he brings the toys to you and is pushy in forcing you to play. In addition, don't pay attention to your Dogo Argentino if he is jumping or biting at you to get attention. Instead, ignore him until he is sitting politely and then give him the attention.

4. Give your Dogo Argentino his own Space

While it can be tempting to keep your dog with you at all times, make sure that you give him his own space as well. Crate training is recommended since it keeps puppies from chewing when you aren't home. You can also give your dog his own bed area.

This area will give him a chance to take a break when the house is too busy or he is tired. In addition, it will be a safe place for him and that will help in establishing roles in your home. Not only will he feel secure in such a place, but also with his role in the house.

5. Always have Access to his Food

Finally, always make sure that you have access to your dog's food dish. When he is a puppy, take the time to have your hands in his dish and also make sure that you feed him a few handfuls.

If your Dogo Argentino becomes too pushy when you are in the dish, lift it up and only feed him by hand when he relaxes. You want to make it clear that the food dish belongs to you and he is simply allowed to eat from it.

You also want to teach him that the food will be given back to him so that he has no need to feel that it is lost to him. Always give treats when interacting with the food dish! Have everyone in the house do the food dish exercise. It helps with preventing food guarding or aggression.

Chapter 9: Training your Dogo Argentino

In the end, when you are training your Dogo Argentino, it comes down to being consistent, firm and making it fun. If you do that, along with providing firm, calm insistence on the behavior you want, you will make progress with training your Dogo Argentino.

Training your Dogo Argentino

This section is about the essential cues that your Dogo Argentino should know and how to teach them.

It is also necessary to recognize that dogs do not understand the concept of "No." They do what they do for their own reasons. Trying to tell them that they are wrong for doing it simply doesn't compute. The reason for this is that the word 'no', does not simply mean 'no', it is a negative word thrown at anything one might say 'no' to.

Dogs need the English words we teach them to have only one definite meaning. 'No' has as many meanings as you can think to apply it to. Therefore, it is impossible for a dog to grasp a concept that is so global and all-encompassing in scope. This is the basis of why we no longer correct dogs for improper performance.

We recommend using a small treat that is soft and does not require a lot of chewing for training. Hard treats that need to be chewed break the training session regularly. The dog has to focus more on chewing than on training.

Chicken nuggets or Frankfurters make excellent small treats. Slice them into pieces that are no larger than half the size of your small finger nail. These treats are rich in flavor, and are easy to chew.

It's important that the treats are small because you don't want your dog to fill up too quickly. You need him to stay hungry long enough to pay attention for the entire time you are training. On the same note, do not feed your dog a big meal just before you start to train him or he won't be interested in your treats. In fact, he will probably feel like taking a nap.

Chapter 9: Training your Dogo Argentino

This part is critically important: You must avoid baiting or bribing your Dogo Argentino into anything except when first learning a behavior. As soon as he grasps what is being asked of him, remove all treats from your hands. You can achieve this by using a treat pouch when you are out or keeping treats high up on shelving when you are home. This is necessary because the dog must be willing to work for a reward and this takes time to teach.

If you continue to bribe a dog for performing, his performance will become dependent on the presence of the bribe. This will not occur if your dog understands the concept of rewards and can trust you to reward him once he has done something right. Performance need not be dependent on the presence of food.

When you are training your Dogo Argentino, keep him on the leash the entire time unless you are practicing off-leash lessons. This will prevent him from wandering away when he is bored. (Hopefully your dog won't get bored with your lessons.)

In addition, never give the cue more than once. If you do this, your Dogo Argentino will decide that he doesn't have to listen.

Essential Cues

"Sit!"

"Sit" is one of the first cues your Dogo Argentino will need to learn. To train "sit," do the following:

1) Have your dog stand in front of you so he is facing you.

2) Place a treat in your right hand and place it near his nose. Do not let him pounce at the treat.

3) Give the cue, never repeat it, and just say it once, "Sit."

Chapter 9: Training your Dogo Argentino

4) Take the treat up and over his head slowly. His muzzle should follow and his bottom should drop. Use the click or the marker word to tell him he is right the instant his bottom touches the ground

5) BE PATIENT, it may take a while to achieve the behavior you want. NEVER force your Dogo Argentino to do anything as this will engage his oppositional reflex and this will shut down any learning that might have occurred.

6) Just be patient and persistent. If it just isn't working, come back to it after a relaxing break.

7) Never punish or correct your Dogo Argentino for an incorrect behavior. This will sour him on the learning experience and can lead to very serious behavioral issues later in life.

If you are having too much difficulty teaching your Dogo Argentino the necessary cues, please contact a Certified Professional Dog Trainer for help.

"Stay!"

"Stay" is another cue that is taught when your puppy is young. It is an important cue that can be used in conjunction with a number of different cues. To train "stay", do the following:

Ask for a "sit" and reward when you receive one. Say the cue word, "Stay" and place your hand in front of his nose, palm facing the dog. Count one second and click or say the marker word and give a treat. Gradually increase the duration of the "stay" by waiting three or four seconds between giving the cue and marking then treating. Once he has completed the "stay" successfully several times, start adding distance in by taking a small step backward after you give the "stay" cue.

1) If he doesn't move, take a step back and praise him, touch his collar and treat him.

Chapter 9: Training your Dogo Argentino

2) Repeat the process, slowly going further away from him and making him wait for longer as the training progresses.

If he breaks the "stay", do not correct or punish, simply reset the "stay" at an easier level and then work the treats back in. Your calm persistence and clear communication will pay off.

"Down"

Teaching "down" refers to teaching your Dogo Argentino to lie down. This should be taught after your dog has learned the "sit" cue since you will often put them into a "down" from a "sit," especially when they are first learning the cue. To train "down," do the following:

1) Ask the dog for a "sit" so he is facing you. Mark and reward that "sit".

2) Place a treat in your right hand and place it near his nose. Do not let him reach for the treat. Slowly move the treat from his nose to his front toes. He should fold right into a down after a few tries. If you are not having any success, just be patient and stick with it. Your persistence will pay off.

3) When he finally does put his front elbows on the floor, mark the behavior with a click or the marker word and deliver a treat. Repeat several times.

4) When the dog has grasped this maneuver, name the behavior with the "Down" cue. To do this, just say the word "down" as you are clicking or marking on the instant the front elbows touch the ground and the dog is lying down.

5) Gradually begin to say the "down" cue sooner, just before the elbows touch the ground. Continue to click or mark and treat as soon as his elbows touch the ground. As the dog is more successful, begin to say the "down" cue sooner and sooner.

Chapter 9: Training your Dogo Argentino

In no time, you will have a good grasp of the "down" cue.

6) Remember, this can take weeks of trying for some Dogo Argentinos to learn. Never use force to mould a Dogo Argentino into position.

7) When he is lying down, give the dog praise, touch his collar and treat him.

"Come"

This is one of the most important cues that you can teach your Dogo Argentino, and is also one of the hardest. This is the cue where you will need to have some trust in your dog. However, when you are first training your Dogo Argentino, you will need to keep him on the leash.

When you are teaching "come," it is important to never use the cue for punishment. What this means is that you should never tell your Dogo Argentino to "come" when he has done something wrong, and then punish him when he does. He will learn that "come" is a bad thing and won't "come" at any other time.

Instead, make it the most wonderful thing that your dog can do. Heap praise on him and give him lots of treats. To encourage your Dogo Argentino to "come", clap your hands, be exciting and interesting and he will come running.

You can train "come" in two different ways, one is when you place him in a "sit" and "stay," and then call him to "come." This is a focused "come" and while it is useful, it shouldn't be the only way you teach "come." Remember that 90% of the time, your dog will need to come when there is something more interesting to look at.

The other way to train "come" is when he is distracted. This can be taught on a leash as well. To do any type of leash training to "come," you should do the following:

Chapter 9: Training your Dogo Argentino

1) Place your dog on the leash. Either have him do a "sit"-"stay" or let him forage out ahead of you. I recommend using a 50-foot lead for this so you can introduce "come" at different distances.

2) If he is in a "sit"-"stay," walk away from the dog and then give the cue for "come." If he is forging ahead, wait until your Dogo Argentino is distracted.

3) Give the cue, "come," and then encourage the dog to come to you by clapping your thighs, being excited and so on. Wave a treat out for him. Do not repeat the cue.

4) Simply walk in the opposite direction. This may pull the leash tight, but remember, once the dog decides to join you, shower him with praise and treats.

5) When the dog reaches you, either on his own or by being reeled in, use the treat to guide him into a "sit" without giving the cue.

6) Praise the dog, touch his collar and treat.

7) Continue training "come" over several weeks. After your puppy becomes adept at "come" at a few feet, increase the distance slightly. The goal is to work up until he can be 100 or more feet from you and still "come" when called, whether on the leash or off.

"Heel"

Many owners have problems with dogs that drag them down the street, pulling their arms out of their sockets, and tangling leashes around legs. It can be dangerous to take a walk with some dogs because of this.

Heeling and walking on a loose leash are two different things. Heeling is more formal and it requires the dog to walk politely at your left side, at knee-level, and sit when you stop walking. It is a cue that is often seen in obedience classes and obedience tests.

Chapter 9: Training your Dogo Argentino

Walking on a loose leash is a more informal cue in which the dog walks politely on the leash without pulling, and is not required to stay exactly by the owner's leg, or to sit when the owner stops walking, but he must not pull on the leash or be rambunctious. A well-trained dog should be able to heel when asked and always walk on a loose leash at other times.

We'll go over training for both of these cues. Heeling first:

To teach your Dogo Argentino to heel you should do the following:

1) Put him on the leash.

2) Set off walking with him on your left side and give the "heel" cue.

3) You should have a large cooking spoon in your left hand. The spoon should contain peanut butter, cream cheese, or some other soft treat that will stay on the spoon. Keep the spoon raised.

4) Every two or three steps lower the spoon and allow your Dogo Argentino to lick the soft treat. Then raise the spoon. Do not break your stride. Continue walking

5) Stop walking. When you are first teaching this cue, you will need to give your dog the "sit" cue when you stop. Eventually he should sit on his own each time you stop.

6) When you stop and your dog sits, let him lick the spoon again. Praise him.

7) Give the "heel" cue and start walking again. Repeat.

This is a very popular method of teaching dogs to heel, and it works. Your dog will be glued to your side while you have that spoon – long enough to learn the cue and what it means. You can gradually stop using the spoon and the soft treat. This method is a lot more fun for your dog than the endless repetitions of the traditional way of teaching a dog to heel, or using a corrective collar.

Chapter 9: Training your Dogo Argentino

Walking on a loose leash

Walking on a loose leash is not a cue as much as it is an expectation. We all expect our dogs to have good manners. This includes when we are out in public with them, walking down the street or visiting someone.

Leash skills begin in puppyhood. This is where your puppy will learn what a leash is and how to behave while on it and off it. There are several rules to follow when teaching a puppy basic leash manners.

First, understand that the leash works both ways. Yet it should never be used as a communication device by jerking or hauling the puppy around with it. If you jerk or haul with the leash, the puppy will learn that the leash means negative actions are on the way.

Second, always treat the leash like a piece of thread; as if it will snap if it is pulled too hard either by the puppy or by you. This will establish an understanding between you and your puppy that goes something like this. "I won't pull the leash too hard if you don't pull the leash too hard." Once this is understood, everything else becomes much easier.

Finally, refrain from using your arm muscles to manipulate the leash. Instead, it is much better to plant your hand in one position (such as your belt line) and use your body to communicate motion to the dog. This is because dogs rarely pay attention to anything above our abdomens. Therefore, it is more effective to use your feet and legs to communicate what you want the puppy to follow, than it is to move your arms.

There are several variations of teaching your dog to walk on a loose leash, and they all use the same principle, that is, keep your dog guessing. Here is the most basic version.

Chapter 9: Training your Dogo Argentino

The Three Iron Rules of Loose Leash Walking

There are only three simple rules to follow for loose leash walking.

1) The dog must never be allowed to get away with pulling. If there is pulling, stop the forward motion immediately. The dog may only go forward if he does it nicely.

2) If pulling continues, walk backwards. The dog must learn that pulling gets him the opposite of what he wants. Be careful to never jerk or use your arm muscles to pull the leash. Your rearward motion will do a much better job of convincing the dog to join you.

3) Success depends on utter consistency. If you decide that the dog can pull because you are heading in that direction anyway, you've just ruined whatever progress you might have made and you must now start again, back at the very beginning.

Advanced Cues

Once your dog has started learning some of the basic cues, you can start adding in some of the more advanced cues. These cues are often useful in everyday life or if you intend to get involved in dog events and activities.

Some of these cues include:

a) Focus or Watch Me

b) Drop it

c) Leave it

These are covered below, and are just a few of the cues you can teach your dog once he knows the basics. You can teach him a wide variety of cues, depending on what you are interested in doing with your dog.

Chapter 9: Training your Dogo Argentino

"Focus" (This should ideally be the dog's name).

Not everyone teaches "focus" but it's useful because it is just a quick reminder to the dog that they need to focus on their handler. To teach "focus," all you need is a treat.

1) Have the dog sit or stand in front of you.

2) Place a treat in your hand and place it against his nose. Do not let him take it.

3) Raise the treat slowly to your face, near your eyes.

4) Give the cue, his name or "Focus" or "Watch."

5) When he glances in your eyes, praise and then give the treat.

6) Remove the treat from your hand and continue rewarding for eye contact. You should practice this in different locations, such as the dog park or in your yard. Be sure to remember that he does not have to "come," he just has to pay attention to you. It is acceptable to toss your treat to the dog if he has paid attention to you at distance.

"Drop It!"

"Drop it" can be a life saving cue since it will teach your Dogo Argentino to drop anything that you do not want him to have. "Drop it" is quite easy to teach but you need to set your dog up for the exercise or wait for him to have something that you need to take. To train "drop it," do the following:

1) Have the dog grab something with his mouth. Playing fetch is a great way to encourage this.

2) Once he has something in his mouth, grab it with one hand. In the other, have a treat.

3) Give the cue, "drop It."

Chapter 9: Training your Dogo Argentino

4) Place the treat near his nose so he can smell it. He should drop the item.

5) If he does, praise and treat.

6) If he does not drop it, stuff the treat in his mouth behind the object, this will get him to drop it.

7) When he drops the item, act like he did it without having food inserted into his mouth; praise and treat.

"Leave It!"

"Leave it," like "drop it," is another cue that could save your dog's life. Teaching them to leave things alone on the ground will keep them from eating dangerous items on walks. To teach "leave it," you want to work in stages. Start by leaving things in your hands and then moving up to leaving things on the ground.

1) Place a treat in your hand and close your fist.

2) Hold it in front of your dog and give the cue, "leave it."

3) Allow him to sniff the treat and try to get at it but ignore him when he is doing this.

4) Once he stops, even for a second, praise the dog and give him a treat with your other hand. Do not give the treat from the hand you told him to leave.

5) Repeat.

6) Increase the difficulty as your dog improves with the cue. Place the treat on your open hand, then on the ground under your cupped hand, and then on the ground without your hand covering. Always treat the dog when he visibly leaves the treat when you give the cue.

Chapter 9: Training your Dogo Argentino

Housetraining

Although we focus on the dog learning to not go inside the house, it is more about training the owner to watch the puppy. The simple fact of housetraining is that a puppy needs to go to the bathroom every few hours, and accidents often happen because owners are not properly watching the dog.

For that reason, it is important to really follow the rules to housetraining. If you follow them, you will find your Dogo Argentino is housetrained very quickly.

1. Keep Watch on your Puppy

The first rule with housetraining is to watch your puppy. Generally, the puppy will give cues, such as sniffing around, going to squat, going to the door, and so on. This will indicate that your Dogo Argentino has to go to the bathroom.

If you are unable to watch your puppy, place him in a crate or somewhere secure where there is non-porous flooring. Generally, puppies will not soil their bed, so if you keep them in their bed when you are unable to watch them, you will be less likely to have an accident.

2. Understand when your Puppy has to Go

Another important rule is to understand when your puppy has to go to the bathroom. In general, puppies will have to go to the bathroom after the following:

a) 5 to 20 minutes after eating or drinking

b) When they first wake up

c) After a play period

d) Every 120 to 240 minutes when awake

Chapter 9: Training your Dogo Argentino

By following this rule and taking your puppy out after each of these common times for them to go to the bathroom, you should be able to prevent 95% of the accidents that might occur.

3. Don't Scold

If you scold your puppy when you see him squatting or peeing, you are likely to scare him into peeing again right away. Nothing positive is accomplished with scolding a puppy that pees in the house. The only thing you have accomplished is making your puppy afraid of you.

Instead, when an accident happens, clap your hands or say, "No" if the dog is in the middle of going to the bathroom. This will break the action and often puppies will stop urinating mid-stream. This is a good time to introduce the concept of an instructive term. Instead of saying "No!" it is a better Idea to say "Outside!" to at least add some instruction to what the puppy should be doing.

As soon as he stops, scoop him up and take him outside immediately. Once he starts again, praise him.

When you are cleaning up the area, place the puppy in his crate and then clean it up where he can't see it.

When you clean up an accident, be sure to clean it up thoroughly. Puppies will always be tempted to return to places where they have eliminated before.

4. Be Persistent

Although it may seem like you are outside all the time, it is important to be persistent. Take your Dogo Argentino outside and wait 3 minutes or until he has gone to the bathroom.

If he hasn't gone to the bathroom after the allotted time, pick him up and place him in his crate. Don't scold or tell him he is bad, simply place him in his crate and reward him for being in his crate. Wait about 5 to 10 minutes and then take him outside again.

Chapter 9: Training your Dogo Argentino

Repeat the process until he has gone to the bathroom. The reason why you are placing him in his crate is to prevent him coming inside and immediately going to the bathroom. When he has finally gone outside and eliminated, praise him and give treats. Be sure not to crate him immediately after this.

5. Praise, Praise and Praise

Finally, make sure you praise your dog. You can wait until he squats outside and starts going to the bathroom, and then the entire time he is going, say, "Good dog, go do your business." "Do your business" becomes a cue for the dog. While your dog won't defecate on cue, when you say, "Do your business," he will know that now isn't the time to sniff around and play and he will go to the bathroom.

For dogs that are harder to housetrain, you can treat them whenever they go outside. This will quickly teach your Dogo Argentino that going to the bathroom outside is a very good thing. As soon as he learns that his urine and feces can be cashed in for tasty rewards, you will have a dog who house trained enthusiastically.

These are the basics of training your Dogo Argentino. Remember that training lasts the life of your Dogo Argentino and you should spend time everyday working on different lessons, even when he is fully trained.

Training your Dogo to Hunt

If you are interested in hunting with your Dogo Argentino, it is a good idea to make this clear to your breeder when you are choosing a puppy. They can do their best in finding you a puppy that shows good hunting instincts. Most puppies should be able to be trained for hunting but some may show more instinct than others. Also verify the rules in your area. For instance, it is rare to find areas that legally allow Dogo-style hunting. The best way to learn how to hunt would be to contact experienced hunters that hunt with Dogos. Your breeder or Breed Club will be able to provide you with assistance in this area.

Chapter Ten: Feeding your Dogo Argentino

Although feeding your Dogo Argentino does not have to be any more complicated than simply pouring dog food into a bowl, it can be beneficial if owners understand dog food and feeding.

Providing your dog with the best possible diet combined with the right amount of activity will help your dog stay healthy, but also look good.

Additionally, avoiding foods with a lot of fillers and chemicals by buying high quality foods will help reduce the risk of some health problems.

Chapter 10: Feeding your Dogo Argentino

Types of Food

When we are looking at feeding a Dogo Argentino, it is important to look at the various foods that you can offer your dog. There are hundreds of different dog food brands available so it can be a little overwhelming when you're trying to select one.

Many people like grain free dog foods today. Grain free foods have some benefits but they are misunderstood by many dog owners. You can also find good quality dog foods that contain some grains. As long as your dog does not have an allergy or food sensitivity to a particular grain, there is no reason to avoid it.

Some dogs do have problems with corn, wheat, or soy, but dogs are more likely to be allergic to ingredients such as beef, chicken, lamb, fish, and even eggs and dairy. These are all common ingredients in dog food. In truth, only a small percentage of dogs have food allergies.

You can generally identify good quality foods by the following factors:

a) Fewer grains (but not necessarily grain free)

b) Lower carbohydrates

c) Two or three named meats in the first several ingredients

d) Named fats

e) No artificial preservatives, flavorings, sweeteners, or colors/dyes

f) No ingredients with "digests;" better foods contain no meat by-products

g) Human grade ingredients are preferred (though, legally, this is controversial since pet food cannot be sold as human food; but the ingredients should be fit for human consumption before they are made into pet food)

Chapter 10: Feeding your Dogo Argentino

In the United States, pet foods should have AAFCO approval (Association of American Feed Control Officials), indicating that they have passed minimum nutritional standards. In Europe, the EU Commission and other entities provide pet food regulations.

In general, most dogs do best on a diet that is high in protein and which has moderate fat. . Large and giant breeds, and especially giant breed puppies, need to have food that is slightly lower in calories. Puppies need to grow slowly. Fast growth can lead to arthritis and other joint problems when the dog is older.

Whenever you change food, whether you are feeding a puppy or an adult dog, you need to do so slowly, over several days to avoid stomach upset. You will need to feed your puppy the food he has been used to eating at the breeder's home at first and then slowly make any changes to his diet.

There are actually four types of food that you can feed your dog. With dog food brands, it really is about doing research and finding the right dog food for you and your Dogo Argentino.

Dry Food

The most common and least expensive food that you can give your dog is dry food. This includes pellets, flaked food, mixes, biscuits, and kibbles. Kibble is very popular. It is easier to store and, per pound, it is often the best choice.

Wet Food

Wet food is food that usually comes in a can and has the consistency of canned fish. It has a very high moisture level and is usually higher in calories than dry food. It can be more expensive than dry food.

Wet food is not practical for many people with large dogs or for people who have lots of dogs because of the cost per ounce and the fact that they would have to feed their dogs numerous cans per day. It can be a

Chapter 10: Feeding your Dogo Argentino

good choice for someone feeding a single Dogo Argentino. However, you can use it as a topping for your dog's kibble or as a special meal. If you give it to your Dogo Argentino, remember to adjust the amount of kibble you are feeding. Otherwise your dog could develop a weight problem.

Semi-moist Food

Semi-moist food comes in small pouches and usually has a kibble-like shape in a meaty gravy. Like wet food, it is usually more expensive than dry. It is usually given as a treat for a dog since it is quite expensive, though some Dogo Argentino owners may choose to feed it as a meal.

Like wet, it works well when you blend it with dry food as a topping or treat.

RAW/Homemade Food

The final type of food that you can give your dog is RAW food or a homemade diet. RAW has a lot of benefits including giving your dog high quality nutrients and a lot of variety. You can tailor the food to your individual Dogo Argentino's needs and you can change it slightly to add in fruits and vegetables.

In addition to the variety, dogs tend to digest more of the RAW diet than they do with the dry kibble so it means less waste to be picked up.

The downside to RAW is that there can be some risk of bacterial poisoning if the food is not properly cooked or stored. In addition, if you are creating the recipes yourself, you could end up with nutritional deficiencies in your Dogo Argentino.

It is important to do a lot of research before feeding any type of food. Make sure that it is whole, of a good quality, and free of chemicals. If you do that, your dog should be healthy.

Chapter 10: Feeding your Dogo Argentino

Feeding

Feeding your Dogo Argentino can be quite easy. It is important to note that how you feed, when you feed, and how much you feed will be different depending on your dog and the food that you are using.

When to Feed

When to feed depends on the age of your dog and also on your schedule. With new Dogo Argentino puppy owners, you should feed your puppy three times per day: once in the morning, once around lunch-time, and once in the evening.

As your puppy grows, you can begin to omit the lunch feeds and move to two meals a day. You can feed one meal a day and it is not unhealthy. You just need to have the kind of housing set up wherein the puppy always has access to the food.

While your Dogo Argentino is eating breakfast, get ready for your day and then he will be ready to go outside right before you leave for work.

In the evening, feed when you arrive home from work, or around dinner time, and he can relieve himself outside before bedtime. Your schedule will determine when you feed your dog, so just keep in mind that he will need enough time to eliminate after.

How much to Feed

Feeding differs depending on the age of your dog, how active the dog is and the type of food you are feeding. High quality dog foods require less food while low quality foods require more, so your dog can reach the necessary caloric intake. With feeding, it is important to look at the weight of your dog, as well as his energy level and age.

To do this, we have to look at the resting energy requirements. What this means is that when your dog is resting, how many calories is the

Chapter 10: Feeding your Dogo Argentino

dog burning? From there, we can begin to adjust the amount of food, or calories that we need to feed the dog.

Determining your dog's resting energy requirements (RER) formula is simple.

RER in kcal/day = 30 (body weight in kg) + 70

Take your dog's weight in kilograms and multiply it by 30. Then add 70. This can also work if you are using pounds but just be sure to convert the weight into kilograms first.

For example, if you have a 23 pound Dogo Argentino, you would divide 23 by 2.2 for a total of 10.45 or 10.5 kilograms, if we round up. Then, multiply 10.5 by 30 for 315 and then add 70 for a total of 385 calories per day. Most dog food bags have the calorie amount for every half cup or cup so you simply divide the calories needed by the calories provided and spread them over the number of meals you are feeding.

For instance, Purina Dog Chow Complete Nutrition has 430 calories for every cup of dog food. So dividing 430 into 385 means that the dog would need slightly more than 3/4 cups of food to meet his caloric intake needs. This is the resting energy requirement for a dog, but they can have a variety of situations. For example, a dog might be pregnant or neutered or have light activity. You can check the chart below to find the number to multiply by your dog's resting energy requirement.

Chapter 10: Feeding your Dogo Argentino

Activity Level/Age	Multiplier for Resting Energy Requirements
Weaning to 4 months	X 3.0
4 months to adult	X 2.0
Lactating female	X 4.8
Pregnant female day 1 to 42	X 1.8
Pregnant female day 42 to whelping	X 3.0
Adult Dog neutered/spayed with normal activity	X 1.6
Adult Dog intact with normal activity	X 1.8
Adult Dog with light activity	X 2.0
Adult Dog with moderate activity	X 3.0
Adult Dog with heavy activity	X 4.8
Adult Dog needing weight loss	X 1.0

As you can see, the daily calories can change depending on the individual dog. So if the same Dogo Argentino from above, that needs 385 calories per day, was a lactating female that was nursing puppies, her calories for the day should be 1848 or 4 1/4 cups of Purina Dog Chow.

Fortunately, most dog food companies have already done this math for you. The guidelines that they include on their labels are based on these figures so you can use their suggestions for how much to feed your dog as a starting point. You will need to watch your puppy or dog when you start feeding him a dog food, to see if he is gaining or losing weight and his overall condition. You can make adjustments to his portions accordingly.

Chapter 10: Feeding your Dogo Argentino

When we are looking at RAW feeding, the amounts are slightly different. In addition, it is difficult to determine the calories as it will be different with the food you are giving.

A pound of beef with 30% blend of organ, meat and bone has about 2600 calories in it, so the Dogo Argentino that weighs 23 pounds only needs about 0.2 pounds of food per day. The reason for this is because the multiplier for the resting energy requirements is higher when feeding raw, which is outlined in the chart below.

Activity Level/Age	Multiplier for Resting Energy Requirements
Weaning to 4 months	X 6.0
4 months to adult	X 4.0
Lactating female	X 8.0
Pregnant female day 1 to 42	X 4.0
Pregnant female day 42 to whelping	X 6.0
Adult Dog neutered/spayed with normal activity	X 2.0
Adult Dog intact with normal activity	X 2.5
Adult Dog with light activity	X 3.0
Adult Dog with moderate activity	X 3.5
Adult Dog with heavy activity	X 4.0
Adult Dog needing weight loss	X 1.5

How to Feed

When we talk about how to feed, it isn't just putting the food into a bowl. Instead, what we are talking about is whether to free feed or not. If you are not sure what free feeding is, it is when you place the dog's food in a dish and allow him access to it constantly.

Chapter 10: Feeding your Dogo Argentino

While this may seem like a great idea, and your dog may like it, it's not advisable in multi-dog households. Free feeding can lead to weight loss if you have other pets in the home that are eating all the food.

Instead of free feeding, make set mealtimes for feeding. Pour the desired amount into the bowl and then give the dog 20 minutes to finish it. If the dog hasn't finished his meal, pick it up and save the food for his next meal-time.

If your dog doesn't eat his meals at first, he will eventually (unless something is medically wrong). Feeding in this manner will allow you to keep track of his calorie intake. Resource guarding, as it is more properly named has nothing to do with free-feeding.

Watering your Dogo Argentino

A Dogo Argentino should be offered water throughout the day and it should be adjusted according to the season. They will drink more water during the hot summer months than during the winter.

Water should be cool but be careful with ice cold water, as too much of it can lead to digestive problems with your Dogo Argentino.

Young puppies that are not fully housetrained should only be offered water at set times. This will help reduce the number of times the puppy has to go to the bathroom. Another rule with young dogs is to pick up the water dish about 2 hours before you go to bed. This will help your puppy make it through the night without an accident.

With adult dogs, or housetrained dogs, you can leave the water down all the time.

To determine if your dog has enough water in the day, you should follow the rule of weight. In general, you should give your dog 1 ounce of water for every pound he weighs, or 66ml for every kilogram of dog.

Chapter 10: Feeding your Dogo Argentino

Treats for your Dogo Argentino

Walk through a pet store and you will see that there are hundreds of different treats for your Dogo Argentino. Really, buying a treat for your dog is as simple as walking into a store. But there are a few things to consider before buying treats.

The first thing is that treats are just that - treats. You should never just feed the treats without thinking about the added calories. Yes, even Dogo Argentinos need to watch their waistlines and feeding treats freely can lead to obesity in your dog. It's estimated that over 50 percent of all dogs are overweight or obese.

A general rule of thumb to follow with treats is to only allow them to take up 10% of your dog's daily calories. In addition, always include the calories as part of your dog's daily caloric intake.

When you are selecting treats for your dogs, follow these rules:

Avoid foods with additives

Avoid feeding your left over foods that have additives in them. Also, never feed your dog from the dinner table as this will reinforce begging.

Choose Natural Ingredients

When you are purchasing treats from the store, read the ingredients label. Only choose foods that have natural ingredients and avoid foods with processed ingredients.

Don't Buy Products Made in China

Although most of the products are safe for your dog, it is important to remember that products made in China do not have all the safety restrictions that they do in other countries. Many products are made with serious chemicals that have been linked to liver disease, cancer and that have even resulted in death.

Chapter 10: Feeding your Dogo Argentino

Try to Use Fresh Foods

While we often think of dog treats as bones or manufactured foods, they can be as simple as giving your dog a carrot. In fact, many fruits and vegetables are safe for your Dogo Argentino and make an excellent treat.

Think of Health Benefits

Finally, when you are choosing your treats, think of health options. Many treats have supplements in them that will help prevent arthritis, boost your dog's immune system and a range of other benefits so check the ingredient list for healthy vitamins and to make sure there are no chemicals in the food.

Here's a list of healthy snack choices for your Dogo Argentino:

Apples (remove seeds)	Kale
Applesauce	Lemons
Apricots (remove pits)	Marrow Bones (raw only)
Baby food (all-natural, make sure it is free of salt)	Mint
Bananas	Nectarines (remove pits)
Beef (raw and cooked)	Oatmeal
Beets	Organ meats (heart, liver, kidney, etc.)
Blackberries	Pasta (cooked)
Blueberries	Peaches (remove pits)
Bran cereal	Peanut butter
Bread (avoid nut breads and raison bread)	Pears
Broccoli (safe when fed raw)	Peas
Brussels Sprouts	Pineapple

Chapter 10: Feeding your Dogo Argentino

Cantaloupe	Plums (remove pits)
Carrots	Pumpkin
Cauliflower: safe when fed raw	Rice: cooked only
Celery	Rice cakes
Cheerios cereal	Salmon
Cheese (cheddar is safe)	Spinach
Chicken (remove bones if cooked)	Squash
Corn: safe off the cob	Strawberries
Cottage cheese	Sweet potatoes
Cranberries	Tomatoes
Cream cheese	Training treats
Cucumbers	Tuna
Dog Cookies (homemade and store bought)	Turkey (cooked without bones)
Eggs (when cooked)	Watermelon
Flax seed	Yogurt
Green beans	Zucchini
Honey	

Foods to Avoid

Here are some foods that you should never feed your dog. While some foods are safe for people, there are a range of foods that can have catastrophic effects on your Dogo Argentino if you feed them to him.

Below is a chart that goes over foods you should avoid giving to your dog.

Chapter 10: Feeding your Dogo Argentino

Foods to Avoid	Reasons to Avoid
Alcohol	Can lead to a coma and/or death
Apple Seeds	Seeds contain cyanide and can lead to death.
Artificial Sweetener	Can cause low blood sugar, vomiting, collapse and liver failure.
Avocado	May cause vomiting and diarrhea
Broccoli	When cooked, it can cause gas, which can lead to bloating. Safe when it is raw.
Cat Food	While not harmful, too much cat food can lead to health problems due to the high protein and fat content.
Cauliflower	When cooked, it can cause gas, which can lead to bloating. Safe when it is raw.
Chocolate	Contains caffeine and theobromine and can lead to vomiting and diarrhea. Can lead to death if too much is consumed.
Cooked Chicken Bones	Cooked chicken has bones that can splinter, which can lead to an obstruction or laceration in the digestive system.
Citrus Oil	May cause vomiting.
Coffee	Contains caffeine and can lead to vomiting and diarrhea. Can lead to death if too much is consumed.
Currants	Can cause kidney damage and death.
Fat Trimmings	High fat levels can lead to pancreatitis.
Any fish that has not been de-boned or Bone-in Fish	Bones can lacerate the digestive system. In addition, if fed a fish exclusive diet, it can lead to vitamin B deficiency, which can cause seizures and death. Fish in dog food is fine as long as other nutrients are in the ingredients

Chapter 10: Feeding your Dogo Argentino

	list. Fish skin is also a nutritious treat.
Garlic	In large doses, can cause anemia.
Grapes	Can cause kidney damage and death.
Grape Seed Oil	Can cause kidney damage and death.
Gum	Can cause blockages and contains Xylitol, which can damage the liver.
Hops	Can cause increased heart rate, fever, seizures and sometimes, death.
Human Vitamins	Can damage a dog's liver, kidneys and digestive system.
Macadamia Nuts	Toxin in the nuts can cause seizures and death.
Milk	Along with other dairy products, can cause diarrhea.
Mushrooms	Can cause shock, shut down multiple body systems and can lead to death.
Onions	Can cause anemia.
Persimmons	The seeds lead to intestinal obstructions.
Peaches	The flesh of the peach is fine, but be sure to remove the pit or it can cause an obstruction.
Pork	Contains bones that will splinter, which can lead to an obstruction or laceration in the digestive system.
Plum Pits	The flesh of the plum is fine, but be sure to remove the pit or it can cause an obstruction.
Raisins	Can cause kidney damage and death.
Raw Eggs	Can cause skin and coat problems since it decreases the absorption of biotin.
Rhubarb Leaves	Poisonous, can affect the urinary tract system, digestive system and nervous system.

Chapter 10: Feeding your Dogo Argentino

Salt	Can lead to vomiting, diarrhea, dehydration and seizures. Large quantities can lead to death.
Sugar	Leads to obesity and has been linked to canine diabetes.
Tea	Contains caffeine and can lead to vomiting and diarrhea. Can lead to death if too much is consumed.
Tomato Greens/Plant	Can cause heart problems in dogs.
Turkey	Cooked turkey has bones that will splinter, which can lead to an obstruction or laceration in the digestive system.
Yeast	Can cause pain, gas and can even cause a rupture in the digestive system, which can result in death.

Chapter 11: Dogo Argentino Health

Chapter Eleven: Dogo Argentino Health

Chapter 11: Dogo Argentino Health

Dogo Argentinos are considered to be a healthy breed with very few health problems. That being said, there some diseases that affect the Dogo Argentino and it is important to make sure that you purchase a dog from a reputable breeder.

Generally, a reputable breeder will have the health of the breeding dogs thoroughly tested before they breed them. The tests that are important with the Dogo Argentino are:

a) Hip Dysplasia

b) BAER testing for deafness

By purchasing from a breeder that health tests their lines, you are less likely to run into the hereditary illnesses that can affect the breed.

Even with the best screening, some diseases can still occur. This chapter is about identifying illnesses in your dog as well as common health problems you may see in your Dogo Argentino.

Signs of Illness

Although signs of illness may differ depending on the disease or illness affecting a dog, there are some general signs that you should look out for. When your Dogo Argentino has any of these symptoms, it is important to seek veterinarian care.

One thing that must be stressed with any breed, including the Dogo Argentino, is that often illnesses are sudden and it is very easy for a dog to go from healthy to gravely ill. Make sure you monitor your dog frequently and perform a daily health check on your Dogo Argentino.

Chapter 11: Dogo Argentino Health

Symptoms that your dog may be sick are:

1) Bad Breath

Bad breath is often a sign of some oral problem but it can also be a sign of other diseases. If your dog has bad breath, and there is no root cause for it that you can see, schedule an appointment with your vet.

2) Drooling

Dogo Argentinos can drool occasionally, like any dog, but excess drooling is a tip off that there could be a health problem. If your dog is drooling a lot, make an appointment to see your vet right away.

3) Loss of Appetite

Loss of appetite is often one of the first indicators that something is wrong with your Dogo Argentino. With loss of appetite, it is very important to look at the pattern of eating. If your dog is usually a picky eater, missing the occasional meal should not give rise to concerns.

However, if your dog normally rushes through his food and he suddenly loses interest in eating, this can be an indication of a problem.

In addition, if you have a female that has not been spayed, she may stop eating around her heat cycles. Pregnancy can also lead to a dog not eating as much.

The biggest concern is when your dog is not eating for more than 24 hours, especially if other symptoms are seen.

4) Excessive Thirst

During the cooler seasons, if your Dogo Argentino seems to be drinking large amounts of water, then it could be an indication of disease or dehydration. In general, a Dogo Argentino should drink about an ounce of water for every pound of dog.

5) Changes in Urination

Changes in the color of urine as well as the frequency of urination can indicate a health problem. It is important to note that an increase in urination can be linked to some illnesses while difficulty urinating can indicate other problems.

If you spot blood in the urine, contact your vet immediately.

6) Skin Problems

If your dog's skin is bright red or you see flaking skin, then there could be a problem with his health.

In addition, if the dog is itching a lot, it could have fleas, some type of mite, or the dog could also have allergies. Make sure you check off all the reasons for the skin problems.

7) Lethargy

Dogo Argentinos may like to sleep during the day but they should not be lethargic. Like changes in appetite, make sure that you identify any reasons why your dog is tired, such as being over-exercised. If there are no apparent reasons, contact your vet.

8) Gum Problems

Although we see gum problems as being linked to teeth or gum disease, they can actually be linked to other serious diseases that can affect your Dogo Argentino. Things to look for are:

a) *Swollen Gums:* Swollen gums, when accompanied by bad breath, can indicate gum disease or other oral problems.

b) *Bright Red Gums:* When a dog's gums are bright red, it could be an indication that the dog is fighting an infection. Exposure to toxins is another reason for bright red gums. Or your dog could have heatstroke.

Chapter 11: Dogo Argentino Health

c) *Blue Gums:* With blue gums, what you are seeing is that the Dogo Argentino is lacking oxygen for some reason. Seek immediate veterinary care.

d) *Purple Gums:* Purple gums are often seen when a dog has gone into shock or there is a problem with his blood circulation. The events that have unfolded before you notice the purple gums will indicate whether your Dogo Argentino is in shock or not.

e) *Grey Gums:* The same as purple gums, when grey gums are seen in a Dogo Argentino, it can indicate either poor blood circulation or shock.

f) *Pale Pink Gums:* Pale pink gums can be an indication of anemia in the Dogo Argentino.

g) *White Gums:* Finally, white gums can be an indication of a loss of blood. This loss can be either externally or internally so contact your vet immediately.

As you can see, gums are one of the primary indicators of illness in dogs. If your dog does not have pink gums, but has black instead, you can check his health by looking at the pink portion of his lower eyelid.

9) Changes in Weight

This is something that is not always easy to follow since it means relying on charting his weight, but if you notice unexpected weight loss or weight gain in your Dogo Argentino, there could be an underlying condition.

10) Stiffness of Limbs

Dogo Argentinos are not usually stiff in their limbs. While old age can create some stiffness, there are several diseases that can affect mobility. If you notice difficulty in getting up, climbing stairs or walking, there may be an underlying problem.

Chapter 11: Dogo Argentino Health

11) Respiratory Problems

Whenever you see excessive sneezing, coughing, labored breathing and panting, take note. It could be nothing, but often respiratory problems are an early indication that there is a health problem.

12) Runny Eyes or Nose

If you see any discharge or fluid coming out of your Dogo Argentino's eyes or nose, keep close watch on his symptoms. This can be linked to several conditions including respiratory illnesses.

13) Vomiting and Gagging

Dogs will gag and vomit without being ill. If you see repeated vomiting or the dog has a bowed look and is continually gagging, seek medical help. Vomiting and gagging can be a sign of allergies or could indicate a life-threatening disease.

14) Fluctuations in Temperature

Finally, if you suspect that your Dogo Argentino's health is compromised, it is important to check your dog's temperature. Temperatures that are too high can indicate a fever, which could be a symptom of a serious disease. Low temperature could indicate other problems such as shock.

Check the temperature with a rectal thermometer or an ear thermometer. Make sure that the Dogo Argentino's temperature is between the following:

a) *Rectal Temperature:* Rectal temperatures in dogs should be between 100.5 to 102.5°F (38 to 39.2°C).

b) *Ear Temperature:* Ear temperatures in dogs should be between 100 to 103°F (37.7 to 39.4°C).

Chapter 11: Dogo Argentino Health

If you see a temperature that is lower or higher, seek veterinary help. One exception to the rule of temperatures is in pregnant females. Read Chapter Twelve, on breeding your Dogo Argentino, for more information on this topic.

It is important to note that some symptoms, occurring on their own, may not indicate any problem. However, if your Dogo Argentino has three or more of the symptoms, you should seek medical care for your dog.

Common Health Problems in the Breed

Dogo Argentinos are, in general, a hardy breed. They have a life expectancy of 10 to 12 years. This is much longer than many breeds of comparable size. They tend to have fewer genetic health problems than some other breeds.

Anyone interested in adopting a Dogo Argentino should be aware of these issues and discuss them with a breeder. Find out the health and genetic history of the parents and other related dogs of any puppy you are considering.

a) Hip dysplasia

The dog's hip joint is made up of a ball and socket. Genetics and the environment help determine how the joint fits together. If the joint does not fit right or if it begins to deteriorate, the dog can develop hip dysplasia. Hip dysplasia is one of the most common health problems seen in dogs.

Symptoms

a) Early disease: signs are related to joint looseness or laxity

b) Later disease: signs are related to joint degeneration and osteoarthritis

c) Decreased activity

Chapter 11: Dogo Argentino Health

d) Difficulty rising

e) Reluctance to run, jump, or climb stairs

f) Intermittent or persistent hind-limb lameness, often worse after exercise

g) Bunny-hopping or swaying gait

h) Narrow stance in the hind limbs (back legs unnaturally close together)

i) Pain in hip joints

j) Joint looseness or laxity – characteristic of early disease; may not be seen in long-term hip dysplasia due to arthritic changes in the hip joint

k) Grating detected with joint movement

l) Decreased range of motion in the hip joints

m) Loss of muscle mass in thigh muscles

n) Enlargement of shoulder muscles due to more weight being exerted on front legs as dog tries to avoid weight on its hips, leading to extra work for the shoulder muscles and subsequent enlargement of these muscles

Treatment

Treatment depends on the individual dog and the severity of the condition. In mild cases, you may never know that your dog has any dysplasia. If your dog begins to show stiffness or other signs of arthritis as he gets older, you can talk to your vet about mild painkillers.

You can also provide a heated, comfortable dog bed. It will also be a good idea if you help your dog avoid stairs and other obstacles that might be physically taxing. However, regular light

Chapter 11: Dogo Argentino Health

exercise is good to keep the muscles in shape. Swimming is very good exercise for older dogs and dogs with hip dysplasia. In rare cases a dog might require surgery, but this is not common.

b) Epilepsy

Dogo Argentinos can have seizures. Some are epileptic in nature and others are not. Epilepsy can be genetic or it can occur for unknown (idiopathic) reasons. It is a brain disorder.

Symptoms

Seizures usually have a short aura before they begin. At this time the dog may seem frightened and confused. Some dogs hide or seek comfort. When the seizure starts, the dog will fall on his side, become stiff, chomp his jaws, salivate, urinate, defecate, vocalize, and may paddle with his limbs. These actions usually continue for between 30 and 90 seconds.

Seizures usually occur when the dog is resting or asleep, so they often happen at night or early in the morning. Most dogs have already recovered by the time the owner brings them to the vet.

If your dog has a seizure, you should stay back. Your dog is not aware of you and you could be accidentally bitten.

After the seizure, your dog may be confused. He may wander or pace. He may be very thirsty. Some dogs recover right away but it can take up to 24 hours for a dog to return to normal. Large breed dogs are more likely to have cluster seizures. This is especially true if they have a pattern of epilepsy.

Treatment

Dogs that start having seizures before they are two years old have a good chance of controlling their seizures with medication.

Dogs can take anti-epileptic and anti-convulsant medications.

Chapter 11: Dogo Argentino Health

One of the side effects is a tendency to become overweight. Your dog may need a diet plan to help him with his weight

c) Ectropion

Ectropion is a condition in which the margin of the lower eyelid rolls forward, exposing the haw, or pink part of the eye. Some of the giant breeds are more inclined to this problem, along with a few other breeds. It can occur in dogs less than one year old. It can come and go in some dogs, occurring when they are tired.

Symptoms

a) Protrusion of the lower eyelid, and exposure of the inner lid

b) Facial staining caused by poor tear drainage

c) History of discharge from conjunctival exposure

d) Recurrent foreign object irritation

e) History of bacterial conjunctivitis

Treatment

A topical lubricant or antibiotic ointment, along with good eye and facial hygiene usually helps most dogs. Surgical treatment may be necessary in some cases.

d) Entropion

Entropion is a genetic condition in which a portion of the eyelid is inverted or folded inward. This can cause an eyelash or hair to irritate and scratch the surface of the eye, leading to corneal ulceration or perforation. Entropion is fairly common in dogs and is seen in a wide variety of breeds, including short-nosed breeds, giant breeds, and sporting breeds. Entropion is almost always diagnosed around the time a puppy reaches its first birthday.

Chapter 11: Dogo Argentino Health

Symptoms

In toy and brachycephalic (short-nosed) breeds of dogs, excess tears and/or inner eye inflammation are common signs of entropion. However, in giant breeds, it is more common to see mucus and/or pus discharge from the outer corner of the eyes. In other breeds of dogs, eye tics, discharge of pus, eye inflammation, or even rupture of the cornea are the typical signs of entropion.

Treatment

Underlying irritants should be removed before any attempt is made to correct the problem surgically. In some cases antibiotics or artificial tears can help with the problem but surgery is often required.

e) Reverse sneezing

Also known as reverse sneeze syndrome or pharyngeal gag reflex, it mainly consists of a series of rapid, loud, and forced inhalations through the nostrils, lasting anywhere between ten seconds and two minutes.

Symptoms

Attacks can occur randomly on an unpredictable basis, and the dog will usually have his head extended forward and stand still during this episode, during which time he will appear to be completely normal before and after the attack.

There is no loss of consciousness nor will he collapse, although sometimes his appearance may seem upsetting. Many dogs have these attacks throughout their lifetimes. It is caused by fluid or debris becoming caught under the dog's palate and limiting his ability to breathe.

It is believed that this attack is a conscious act by dogs to remove mucus from the nasal passages, and to add to this, many dogs

Chapter 11: Dogo Argentino Health

swallow at the end of the attack.

Treatment

This condition is usually not serious, but if it appears suddenly in an older dog or if episodes become more severe or frequent, the nasal passages and throat should be examined immediately. If a nasal discharge is found or if a cough takes place, then you should notify your vet as soon as possible.

Treatment is not necessary when the episodes occur infrequently on a random basis.

Home treatments that have been reported to be successful include massaging the throat, blowing in the nose, and rapidly (and lightly) compressing the chest. Another effective treatment is to simply cover the dog's nose with your hands for 3 to 5 seconds and this will normally stop the reverse sneezing.

f) Deafness

Congenital deafness appears in some 80 dog breeds. It is especially likely to occur in breeds with white pigment, such as Dalmatians, English Setters, Bull Terriers, Dogo Argentinos and many others. The merle gene and the piebald gene are thought to be particularly responsible for this problem. The inheritance of genes involving deafness is not always clear cut. However, breeders are advised not to breed dogs that are either unilaterally or bilaterally deaf. On the other hand, unilaterally deaf dogs can make very good pets. Most people do not realize these dogs have any deafness.

Puppies can be tested as early as five weeks at a testing centre or university with the necessary equipment to perform the BAER test and determine if they can hear in one or both ears. It is estimated that about 10 percent of Dogo Argentinos have some degree of deafness.

Chapter 11: Dogo Argentino Health

Sunburn

While not a serious health issue in most cases, dogs with white coats and pink skin, such as the Dogo Argentino, can suffer from sunburn. Take precautions during the summer with these dogs. You may wish to apply a sunblock to their skin, especially to their stomach and other areas where the coat is sparse.

First Aid for your Dogo Argentino

While it's important to work with your veterinarian, you should also be familiar with the basics of canine first aid. You can take several courses that will take you through more in-depth first aid but this section should get you started.

First Aid Kit

Every home that has a Dogo Argentino should have a first aid kit. Having a first aid kit will not only reduce the chance of having to go to the vet's office but will also give your dog precious minutes in a life-threatening situation.

To create a first aid kit, fill an easy-to-access Tupperware or backpack with the following:

1) Important Numbers

Attach important numbers to your first aid kit box, so you never have to search for the number during a crisis. Numbers to have on hand are:

a) Your Veterinarian's Office

b) Emergency Clinic - also have the address to the clinic

c) Poison Control Centre

Chapter 11: Dogo Argentino Health

b) Medicine

There are a number of medications that you can have on hand, which will help you manage a condition or treat it quickly. Always keep track of expiration dates on the medication in your first aid kit.

a) Wound Disinfectant for cuts

b) Sterile Saline for washing out wounds

c) Antibiotic Cream for cuts, scrapes, etc.

d) Cortisone Cream for itchy skin

e) Ear Cleaning Solution

f) Eye Wash Solution

g) Antibiotic Eye Ointment

h) Hydrogen Peroxide for vomiting (only use at the discretion of your vet)

i) Activated Charcoal (only use at the discretion of your vet)

j) Gas X or any gas medication to help prevent bloat

k) Anti-diarrheal medication

l) Benadryl for allergies (only use at the discretion of your vet)

c) Equipment

While you may not feel you need a lot of equipment, you should have the equipment listed below. Sometimes having the right equipment can save the life of your dog, and it can also mean that your dog is treated at home and not at the vet clinic.

Chapter 11: Dogo Argentino Health

a) Magnifying glass

b) Nail clippers

c) Cotton balls

d) Cotton swabs

e) Cold packs

f) Heat packs

g) Thermometer

h) Towels and blankets in case of emergency transport

i) Scissors

k) Penlight

l) Styptic powder (to stop bleeding)

m) Nail clippers

n) Metal nail file

o) Oral syringe

p) Hemostat

q) KY Jelly

r) Eye Dropper

s) Tweezers

t) Disposable gloves

u) Bitter Apple (taste deterrent)

Chapter 11: Dogo Argentino Health

In addition to these items, you should have a crate or pet carrier near your first aid kit for transporting your Dogo Argentino.

d) Bandages and Other

Finally, you will want to make sure that you have bandages and a few odds and ends in your first aid kit. Things you should have are:

a) Karo Syrup

b) Vitacal or other nutritional supplement

c) Gatorade (for rehydration)

d) Band-Aids

e) Square Gauze

f) Non-stick pads

g) First aid tape

h) Bandage rolls

i) Vetwrap

Once you have all your supplies, place the kit in an easy to access area.

Dealing with an Emergency

Now that you have your first aid kit all ready for your Dogo Argentino, you are prepared for many of the little mishaps that life with a dog can bring. But are you ready for an emergency? Hopefully, the answer is yes. In this section we'll go over some of the things you should know.

Chapter 11: Dogo Argentino Health

Here are some tips for dealing with an emergency.

Be Calm and Cautious

Although the first reaction is to panic, remain calm so your dog can feel the strength coming from you. In addition, always be cautious with handling the dog when there's an emergency. If your Dogo Argentino is hurt or frightened, moving too roughly can injure him further or cause him to react.

Only Move Your Dog if Necessary

Make sure that you only move your dog if he needs to be moved. Sometimes lifting a dog too soon can compound the injury. If you can, wrap him carefully in a blanket and then move him.

Use your Voice

Dogo Argentinos often have a very strong bond with their owners and will react to your voice. If you talk to the dog in a loving and gentle manner, the dog will pick up on your tone and relax. This will make first aid or seeking medical help easier.

Keep your Dogo Argentino Warm

Wrap your dog in a warm towel or apply a warm compress if your dog is unconscious or showing any signs of going into shock. By keeping your dog warm, you are less likely to complicate his condition.

Staunch Blood Loss

In the event of an injury with blood loss, make a compression bandage or manually compress the area to prevent as much blood loss as possible.

Remember that what you do in those first few minutes after a serious accident or emergency can mean the difference between life and death in some cases.

Chapter 11: Dogo Argentino Health

First Aid for Eye Injuries

When your Dogo Argentino has an eye injury, it is important to look at the type of injury. If there is something in the eye, carefully flush it with an eye-wash. You may need to have someone hold your dog's head while you put the liquid in the eye.

If your dog has injured his eye and it is bleeding, use an eye-dropper to carefully rinse the eyeball. You do not want to flush but simply moisten it. Once it is moistened, apply a compress gently over the eye. This will help staunch the bleeding and will keep the eye free from exposure.

Seek immediate veterinarian care after you have administered the first aid.

First Aid for Seizures

If your Dogo Argentino has a seizure you should contact your veterinarian as soon as possible. There can be several reasons for a seizure.

During the seizure, don't hold your dog. They can be very scared during a seizure and may bite while having the seizure.

In addition to staying clear, remove any objects that he might hurt himself on, such as furniture. Finally, turn off any type of stimulation. Lights should be turned off, radios as well, and people should try to stay quiet.

While the seizure is happening, time it and write down when it started and when it ended. This is important in case there are recurring seizures.

After the seizure has stopped, comfort your dog. Wrap him in a warm blanket and then sit with him until he begins to act normal. Follow the directions of your vet and take him in for an examination.

Chapter 11: Dogo Argentino Health

First Aid for Heat Stroke

To help prevent heat stroke, do not leave your dog outside when it's very hot. Dogo Argentinos cannot tolerate heat very well. In addition, never leave a dog in a hot car.

If your Dogo Argentino does develop heat stroke, it is important to follow these steps:

1) Move the dog out of the hot area. Bring him to shade or inside.

2) Soak a towel with cold water.

3) Place the towel over the neck and head of your dog. Do not cover his eyes and keep his face clear of the fabric.

4) Repeat the process, wetting the towel down with cold water every few minutes.

5) If you can't get to a vet, pour water over the dog's hind legs and abdomen.

6) While you are pouring water, massage the legs and then push the water off of the dog. Keeping the water moving will help cool the dog more.

As soon as you are able to, take the dog to the veterinarian. Heat exhaustion needs to be treated with the help of a trained professional.

First Aid for Fractures

This is another emergency that will require veterinarian care, as there is not a lot that you can do for your Dogo Argentino if there is a fracture. While some people will try to create a splint, this can cause more harm than good.

Chapter 11: Dogo Argentino Health

Instead, take the time to muzzle your dog to keep him from biting. Then make a sling from a towel and blanket and keep him secure. Do not press on his chest or touch the area where the fracture is.

Place a blanket over him to keep your dog warm, especially if he is going into shock.

Take your pet to the veterinarian's office immediately.

First Aid for Burns

In the event of a burn, as long as it is not a severe burn that covers a large portion of the dog's body, you can treat the burn at home. If it is severe or covers a large area, seek medical attention immediately.

For small burns, flush the burn area with large quantities of water until the burn starts to cool. You can use a burn relief ointment but make sure that it is not toxic if ingested.

First Aid for Choking

Choking can be a very scary situation for dog owners and it can happen very quickly. If your dog is choking, be sure to act quickly but be mindful that a choking dog is more likely to bite.

When the dog is choking, carefully grab his muzzle. Open his mouth and look inside it. If you can see the object that is causing him to choke, take a pair of tweezers and carefully pull the object out.

It is very important to be careful when you are doing this as it is easy to push the object further back into the throat. If you are unable to get the object out, seek medical help immediately.

If your Dogo Argentino stops breathing or collapses, place him on his side. Place your hand over the rib cage and firmly strike the rib cage three to four times with the flat of your palm. Repeat as necessary on your journey to the vet.

Chapter 11: Dogo Argentino Health

While this may have no effect, administering this technique could force the air out of the lungs and force the obstruction out of your dog's throat.

First Aid for Shock

Another emergency that needs medical help is shock, and it should be managed as you take your dog to the vet.

Wrap your dog in a warm blanket and keep him warm. Also, lay him down and try to keep his head level with the rest of his body. Stay calm and comfort your dog to help minimize his discomfort.

First Aid for Bleeding

If your Dogo Argentino has an injury that has resulted in bleeding, it is important to staunch the flow of blood. Using a thick gauze pad, apply pressure to the wound. The pressure will aid in stimulating the clotting mechanism of blood. If it is a minor injury, the bleeding will usually stop in a few minutes and you can then move to cleaning the wound.

If it is severe, keep the pressure on the dog's wound. Wrap him in a blanket or use a heat pad to keep him warm. This will help prevent shock as you take him to the veterinarian for treatment.

First Aid for Poisoning

Finally, if your dog is exposed to poison, it is important to immediately call poison control and/or your vet. They will guide you through the steps to take, depending on the poison he has ingested. In the case of some toxins, you may be advised to administer active charcoal. In cases of consuming poisons, hydrogen peroxide may be recommended to induce vomiting. If it makes contact with the skin or eyes, wash the area or flush it with water.

Chapter 11: Dogo Argentino Health

CPR

CPR should only be used in the event that your dog is not breathing. If he is, do not administer CPR or you could cause more harm than good.

With CPR, follow these steps:

1. Remain calm.

2. Get someone to call your veterinarian.

3. Check the condition of your Dogo Argentino. Is he unconscious?

4. Open your dog's mouth and pull out his tongue until it is lying flat. Check to see if there is an obstruction. If there is, refer to the section on First Aid for Choking.

5. If there isn't, close your Dogo Argentino's mouth and hold it closed. Place your mouth on his nose and breathe.

6. Watch the chest and breathe until it expands.

7. Pause and count to 5, then repeat with a breath.

8. Check your dog's heartbeat. The best place to do this is right above the pad on his front paw.

9. Lay him on his right side.

10. Slip your one hand under his right side in the lower half of his chest.

11. Place your hand, palm down over the lower half of his left side. This is where the heart is on a dog.

12. Press down about a half inch into the chest. (The depth varies with 1 inch (2.5cm) for medium sized dogs, more for larger, less for smaller.)

Chapter 11: Dogo Argentino Health

13. Press down repeatedly, about 100 to 150 times per minute for small dogs, 80 to 120 times per minute for larger ones.

14. If you are using rescue breathing, have someone help you. One person can press the chest for 4 to 5 seconds for every single breath.

15. Repeat until you can feel a heartbeat or do it while someone else is driving you and your Dogo Argentino to the vet.

Although the information in this chapter will help you and your Dogo Argentino, please remember that it should never replace the advice and care of a veterinarian.

Chapter Twelve: Breeding your Dogo Argentino

Breeding your Dogo Argentino is an important decision that every dog owner should make before they purchase a puppy. While we often think of breeding after the purchase, by choosing to breed beforehand, you can ensure that you are starting with the very best dog you can find.

Remember to read the chapter on choosing a puppy in this book. One thing that will help you is to find a mentor in the breed before you decide to breed your dog. Breeding a Dogo Argentino is a constant learning experience and it will help you to know someone in the breed who has years of experience.

This chapter will provide you with tips on choosing the right dogs for your breeding program, how and when to breed, the simple facts about birthing a puppy, and the schedule for raising puppies.

Chapter 12: Breeding your Dogo Argentino

Choosing dogs to breed

As a breed, the Dogo Argentino is less than 100 years old. The breed has a small gene pool and breeding population. Many breeders are dedicated to the breed. They feel strongly that their dogs should not be spayed or neutered if they are of good breeding quality. They want to see them bred and produce the next generation of healthy Dogos. Please keep this in mind if you are interested in getting a Dogo Argentino. Breeding them and working with mentors in the breed is important for the survival of these dogs.

The very first thing that you should do before deciding to breed your Dogo Argentino is to choose the right dogs. **While every dog can be bred, not every dog should be bred**. It is important to really understand the breed standard of the Dogo Argentino before you breed.

If you are interested in breeding professionally, you will probably want to find a "breeding pair" – a registered male and female Dogo Argentino. However, most people who breed as a hobby or breed to show their dogs will look for the best male or female dog they can find. They usually seek the best female dog if they want to breed a litter. That's because they can use stud dogs, owned by other breeders, without tying themselves to the same male forever.

If you have a good female dog, you will likely want to choose a different mate for her each time. That way you can see what kind of puppies she produces with different dogs or different bloodlines. If you are serious about being a dog breeder, you need to think in terms of generations. Having two or three litters from your girl from different bloodlines could give you the best start for the future, assuming you will be keeping a puppy from a litter for yourself.

You should always have the breed's best interest at heart and try to contribute to the Dogo Argentino gene pool. In general, when you are choosing a dog for breeding, you want to look at the following:

Chapter 12: Breeding your Dogo Argentino

Health

Dogs should be healthy and in good condition. They should be in proportionate weight for their build and also pass a health test from your vet. They should be free of disease so there is no risk of that disease being passed along to the young.

If the vet voices any concerns over the health of the dogs, wait to breed them until they are in better health or choose different dogs.

Clearances

Clearances are very important to ensure the health of your puppies and the lifelong health of any dog you produce. Dogo Argentinos have several hereditary diseases so the health clearances you should obtain on your dogs are the following in the United States:

a) Hip Dysplasia

b) BAER testing for deafness

In addition to these clearances, you should have the dogs tested for brucellosis, which is a canine STD. Any dog that is being bred should be clear. Brucellosis can cause sterility in both males and females and can cause the dam to abort the puppies.

Registration

Before buying any dog for breeding, you should make sure the dog is registered with the kennel club you desire, or eligible to be registered.

Temperament

Temperament is as important as health when it comes to breeding. Studies have proven that temperament is a hereditary trait so it is important to breed dogs with a sound temperament. If you have a dog with aggression problems or skittishness, it is recommended that you do not breed the dog.

Chapter 12: Breeding your Dogo Argentino

Bloodlines

Another factor that you want to take into account is the bloodline. Is it a strong pedigree? When considering pedigrees for breeding, it is particularly important to have a mentor or someone you trust to give you some advice. Line-breeding, out-crossing, and other breeding theories, as well as just reading pedigrees takes some practice to understand them. Something to strive for is low COI (coefficient of inbreeding).

Age

The age of the breeding dogs is very important. Females should be no younger than 24 months of age for breeding and males shouldn't be younger than 18 months of age. Ideally, you won't breed a male or female before they have had at least preliminary hip x-rays so you can be reasonably certain they do not have hip dysplasia.

On the other end of the age spectrum, you should not breed a bitch after she is 7 years of age. Males can be bred for many years after that; however, the quality and quantity of sperm can be affected by age.

Physical Traits

Finally, you will want to choose dogs according to their physical traits. While the dogs you select should be good examples of the breed, you should look at what attributes each dog can bring to their future puppies.

For instance, if both dogs have excellent ears according to the breed standard, the odds are very high that the puppies will inherit those ears. A good coat on a female may be passed on to the puppies, even if the male has a coat that isn't as good. A good body shape on the male may be passed on to the puppies and so on.

Choosing complementary traits will only improve your puppies and your lines. While many people promote showing, it is not a prerequisite

Chapter 12: Breeding your Dogo Argentino

for breeding. However, showing your dogs does have benefits for breeding dogs. It puts you in touch with a community of reputable breeders. It allows you to see many Dogo Argentinos and compare traits. It keeps you informed about dog matters. So, it has advantages for anyone interested in breeding dogs.

Choosing a proven stud dog for your girl also has advantages since you can see the puppies and young dogs which the stud dog has already produced. This gives you a hint about what the dog might produce with your girl.

Before you do make that final decision about which dogs to breed, it is important to remember that breeding is a responsibility. There is often very little money to be earned when doing it properly and it is a full time commitment.

While the dam will help with the care, there is a lot to be done during those 8 (or more) weeks that you will be raising puppies at home. In addition, breeders should be prepared to re-home any of their puppies if they are returned for some reason.

Breeding is not for the faint of heart by any means but one thing is certain: cuddling a newborn Dogo Argentino in your arms is worth all the work, money and commitment.

Before breeding your female dog, we recommend that you make sure she is up-to-date on her vaccinations. The mother dog will be able to pass along temporary immunity to common dog diseases to her puppies when they are born so you want to make sure her own immunity is at the best level it can be.

In the UK and Europe we also recommend that mothers receive the canine herpes virus vaccination before breeding. The canine herpes virus is extremely widespread, affecting up to 90 percent of all dogs. It is harmless to most adult dogs but, under stress, it can kill newborn puppies. The vaccine is very helpful in protecting the newborns.

Chapter 12: Breeding your Dogo Argentino

Unfortunately, this vaccine is not currently available in the United States.

Breeding your Dogo Argentino

Now that you have chosen the dogs you wish to breed, it is time to breed your dog. While it may seem like a simple thing, breeding a Dogo Argentino can be challenging. Dogs know how to mate, but there is a lot you need to know to have a successful litter.

The Heat

When a female dog reaches sexual maturity, she will begin what is known as a heat. A heat or heat cycle is when the female will begin bleeding and will be ready to accept the male within a few days. For female Dogo Argentinos, the first heat is usually between six months and a year. However, she should never be bred on her first heat or before the age of 18 months to 2 years.

With heat cycles, some females will take longer to have their first heat and it is not uncommon for a Dogo Argentino to be closer to a year of age or even up to 2 years when she has her first heat. Small dogs often come in season at an earlier age than larger dogs, but not always.

Most female dogs come in season once or twice a year. Depending on the dog and the bloodline, they can come in season anywhere from every six to 14 months or so. Most female dogs are fairly regular in their heat periods once they are mature. However, if you are waiting to breed your girl, they always seem to take longer to come in season.

With heat cycles, signs of the heat begin before the discharge. Often the vulva begins to swell and the female will begin licking her back end and vulva more. In addition, she may be urinating more frequently and if you have any male dogs in the home, you may notice them paying more attention to her than usual.

Chapter 12: Breeding your Dogo Argentino

The female will begin to have a bloody discharge and this can vary in heaviness between females and even heats. Some females have very little discharge and other females have a lot. **Females are not ready to breed at this time.** The discharge will gradually become paler until it is a straw color. This usually takes around 2 to 11 days. This is when the female is ready to breed.

Young male dogs may not be able to tell the difference but experienced stud dogs often won't bother spending much time with a female until she is actually ready to breed.

The entire heat cycle lasts about 3 weeks but it is important to not let the female near a male until about 4 weeks after the start of her heat. If you are planning on breeding her, breeding will take place about 9 to 11 days after her heat starts.

Natural or Artificial?

When you are breeding, you can choose between allowing your dogs to breed naturally, and opting for an AI (Artificial Insemination) breeding. Many breeders learn how to do AIs themselves. However, in the event of frozen sperm, you would need to have the AI done by a veterinarian, specifically a reproductive veterinarian.

Frozen sperm is often shipped from one breeder to another, at a considerable expense. You don't want to take any chances that the insemination might fail.

Natural breeding is when you allow the male dog to mount the female and achieve a tie. This is often the more preferred way to breed.

With AI, the sperm is delivered to the vagina through a sterilized tube. There are several reasons why you would use AI and these are:

a) Stud dog is too far away.

b) A dominant female that will not allow a male to mount.

Chapter 12: Breeding your Dogo Argentino

c) Inexperienced stud dog.

d) A persistent hymen in a bitch.

e) Size incompatibility.

AI is less likely to spread an STD but it usually accounts for smaller litter sizes. Also, it is important to properly judge when ovulation occurs, which can be difficult and is usually done with progesterone testing by your vet.

Many breeders use AI with fresh semen, even when the stud dog is on the premises. This is done to avoid any injury to the stud dog and to avoid any chance of passing disease.

When to Breed

You have the stud dog, a bitch in heat and you have made the decision to go with a natural tie. Terrific, you are ready to start breeding soon ... but maybe not right away.

Breeding times differs from female to female, although the general rule of thumb is between days 9 and 11. If you have the male in the home, you can begin breeding as soon as the female starts accepting him.

However, the rule of thumb is to breed every other day. This gives the sperm time to recover in numbers and you will have better sperm numbers.

If you don't have a male, you can do progesterone testing to try to narrow down when your female is most fertile. Progesterone testing is done via a blood test. However, a vaginal smear can also be used as an indicator, although this is not as accurate.

When using progesterone testing, follow the guidelines of your veterinarian.

Chapter 12: Breeding your Dogo Argentino

Although testing the dog is an excellent way to identify if your female dog is ready to be bred, you can also see this with her behavior. A female that is ready to be bred will exhibit the following:

a) Vaginal discharge will turn to a light pink or straw color.

b) The female will back up into the male.

c) She will hold her tail to the side. This is known as flagging.

d) She will be playful with the male.

e) She will stand still when the male is sniffing her.

f) She won't attack the male when he tries to mount her.

When you see these signs, your female is ready to be bred. However, even with these signs, progesterone testing can be more accurate for determining the exact right time for mating. There is a spike in the LH (luteinizing hormone) 48 hours prior to ovulation. This spike will trigger the progesterone levels to begin rising, signaling the best times for breeding.

After the LH surge and the rise in progesterone, do a natural breeding three days later. The sperm in fresh semen can survive 5 to 7 days in the female dog's uterus.

Artificial insemination using fresh chilled semen can be used four days after the rise in progesterone. Sperm in chilled semen survive 48 to 72 hours after insemination.

Artificial insemination using frozen semen can be used five days after the progesterone surge. Sperm in frozen semen only survives 24 hours once it is deposited in the uterus by surgical means after insemination.

Chapter 12: Breeding your Dogo Argentino

The Act of Breeding

When your female is ready to be bred, it is time to let the dogs do their job. During this time, you should allow the stud dog and the bitch to be together. Never leave them unattended as injuries can occur if the female attacks the male or she becomes scared.

The stud dog will spend some time sniffing the rear of the female and he may begin to lick the vulva. The female will stand still and will move her tail out of the way. She will also back into the male.

Note, if you have a maiden bitch or an inexperienced stud dog, you can have success without intervening, but things often go much better if you are on hand to assist. For example, inexperienced stud dogs can sometimes be so excited that they will mount the wrong end of the girl.

The dogs usually figure things out but if you have invested a lot of money in a stud fee or driven a long way with your girl, sometimes it helps if you or the stud dog owner can lend a guiding hand. For example, you can hold the bitch in position or guide the boy in the right direction.

If you have an experienced bitch and/or stud dog, they usually know what they are doing and things go smoothly and quickly when the time is right.

As the male builds excitement, he will mount the female, wrapping his front legs around the hips of the female. He will begin to thrust against the female and his penis will enter the vulva.

During this action, the glans penis will come out of the sheath, which is a bright red organ. The penis will extend into the vulva until the dog locks with the female. Once the lock happens, the male and female cannot be separated. Do not try to separate them as you can hurt both the male and the female.

Chapter 12: Breeding your Dogo Argentino

Once he is locked, the male will lift his leg over the rear of the female and then turn so they are standing with their back ends together. The penis will bend but will still be inserted in the vulva.

Dogs will remain locked for 10 to 30 minutes until the penis loses some of its swelling so it is released from the lock.

One myth is that a female cannot get pregnant if there is no tie. This is not true. When the dog is thrusting, sperm is released. The fluid that is released when they are locked is very low in sperm and is used to push the sperm through the cervix. Only allow your dogs to mate once per day and then wait a day before you breed again.

Is She Pregnant

The gestational period for dogs is between the 63 to 65 days after the time of first breeding. However, you can have some additional or fewer days depending on the individual dog and breeding. If you have used progesterone testing, whelping is nearly always exactly 63 days after ovulation. Even if you have bred your dogs late in the heat, you can count on 63 days from ovulation rather than from the date of the breeding.

One of the biggest worries that breeders go through is whether a dog is pregnant. This is very difficult to determine because a female dog goes through the same hormone changes whether she is pregnant or not. In fact, even a female that has not been bred can present the symptoms of pregnancy.

During the first month, you will notice very few signs. The female may have morning sickness where her appetite decreases. However, some females are not affected at all.

After the first 30 days, the dog will begin to show some symptoms. Symptoms of pregnancy are:

a) Nipple Growth

Chapter 12: Breeding your Dogo Argentino

b) Pinking of the Nipples

c) Decreased Appetite early on

d) Increased Appetite around week 6

e) Clinginess and other behavior changes

f) Pear shape of the abdomen

g) Weight gain

At 30 to 35 days, you can have an ultrasound done to confirm pregnancy. Numbers are not usually given during ultrasounds as it is very difficult to count the puppies. Experienced vets and breeders can often palpate a bitch's abdomen and feel puppies. At 30 days, puppies are about the size of walnuts. After this time they can't be felt again for several weeks.

After 45 days gestation, an x-ray can be done and the puppies can be counted at that time. It is important to note that sometimes counts are wrong since puppies will hide in the x-ray. It is a good idea to have an x-ray done so you will know how many puppies to expect. This helps you know when your girl is finished whelping.

During pregnancy you can continue to feed your female her normal dog food for the first six weeks. After this time you can begin to increase her food. You can add some pre-natal vitamins to her diet but do **not** add any additional calcium or other supplements at this time.

You can switch her to an all life stage dog food or a puppy food at this time since she will be using the extra calories as the puppies develop. Once the puppies are born, you can feed your female dog as much as she wants to eat, especially if she has several puppies. She will need the extra calories to produce milk.

Chapter 12: Breeding your Dogo Argentino

Whelping your Pups

So your female is pregnant and the time is drawing closer to you whelping her puppies. This is an exciting time but it is also a busy time for you. It is very important to have all your supplies ready and to begin preparing for the puppies a few weeks before their arrival.

Whelping Supplies

It is important to have the whelping supplies on hand. These are essential for helping your puppies and mother.

In the best case scenario, you will need to interact very little with the labor. In the worst case, you could be looking at having to rush your pregnant dog to the vet clinic for an emergency c-section.

Even an easy whelping can result in puppies in distress so it is important to have the tools on hand to help the puppies. Things you will need in your whelping supplies are:

a) Whelping Box: This should be a square box that the mother can deliver and raise her puppies in. You can make the box yourself or you can purchase pre-made whelping boxes. The box does need to be sturdy and good quality. This will be the puppies' home for the next few weeks.

b) Blankets: Have a lot of blankets on hand for your whelping box. Labor is messy and that means you have to exchange the bedding in the whelping box several times during labor.

c) Newspaper: In addition to blankets, have a large amount of newspaper to put down during the whelping process. Again, you are going to be getting through a lot of it. You can also purchase end rolls from your local newspaper outlet. These are clean paper rolls without the ink. They aren't nearly as messy as newspaper.

Chapter 12: Breeding your Dogo Argentino

d) Basket: A laundry basket or Tupperware container to put the puppies in when the female is birthing another puppy.

e) Hot Water Bottles: Water bottles are needed for the basket so puppies can stay warm when they are not with their mother. Puppies will cuddle up to the water bottles if they are cold and will move away if they are too warm. You can also use a heating pad, but wrap it with a towel so the puppies don't get burnt.

f) Scale: Have a kitchen scale so you can properly weigh each puppy as it is born. This will be a tool you use throughout the time the litter is with you since you will want to weigh the puppies on a regular basis.

g) Notebook and Pens: Create a notebook that charts the progress of each individual puppy. Start with the puppies' sex, identifier, date-of-birth, presentation at birth, time born, coloration and weight. This will help you keep track of each puppy.

h) Identifier: This can be yarn, puppy collars, or nail polish for their nails. Basically, it is anything that you can use to identify each puppy. Use the yarn like a collar on each puppy so you can identify each individual puppy right from birth. Use the same collar color for that puppy throughout the 8 weeks that you have the puppies.

In addition to those items, have the following items available in a kit. Be sure to sterilize all of the instruments such as the scissors and hemostats:

a) Sharp Scissors

b) Hemostats

c) Surgical Gloves

d) Iodine Swabs

e) Alcohol Swabs

Chapter 12: Breeding your Dogo Argentino

f) Lubricating Jelly such as K-Y

g) Digital Thermometer

h) Vaseline

i) Nursing Bottles for Puppies

j) Liquid Puppy Vitamins

k) Puppy Formula

l) Energizing Glucose Drops

m) Bulb Syringe

Place all of the items into an easy to access container and have it close to your whelping box.

Before Labor

As you know, the gestation period for dogs is about 63 days, give or take a few days. However, it is important to monitor your dog during the days leading up to the delivery. Around day 56 to 58, the female should start searching for a nesting site. Encourage her to nest in the whelping box by sitting next to it and calmly petting her. Don't discourage her scratching at the bedding as this is normal.

In addition to this, you should start taking her temperature about a week before her due date. The average temperature of your female will be between 99 to 101°F (37.22 to 38.33°C). Mark down her temperature each day and, closer to the due date, start checking her temperature several times per day.

The reason why we are watching the temperature is because we are waiting for a temperature spike and then drop. About 48 hours before labor, her temperature will have a spike up to about 101.5°F (38.6°C) or higher. Within 24 hours after that, the temperature will drop. Once it

Chapter 12: Breeding your Dogo Argentino

gets to below 98°F (36.7°C), you will have between 12 to 24 hours before the litter is expected.

First Stage Labor

When she has her final temperature drop, you will start to notice a number of signs that signal her going into labor. For about 2 to 12 hours, your female will become restless. She may start to nest even more than she did before, or she may become very stressed, wanting to wander around the house.

You may see some shivering and she will probably change positions frequently. Her eyes will dilate and she will watch you and want to be with you. Try to stay near the whelping box so she can settle in.

She may lose her appetite during this time and it is not uncommon for your female Dogo Argentino to vomit. Also, she may try to go to the bathroom and not be able to. This is caused by the pressure building up in her stomach.

If you take your Dogo Argentino outside to go to the bathroom, keep her on a leash and check the spot where she squatted. It is not uncommon for puppies to be born outside.

Finally, you may see some mucus being discharged from the vulva.

Second Stage of Labor

During the second stage of labor, your female should start digging at her bedding even more. You will also notice your Dogo Argentino looking at her back end more frequently and she may start licking her vulva.

Shivering is more noticeable and she will have periods where she is panting heavily. You may be able to see mild contractions going across her belly or you may feel a tightening of her stomach.

Chapter 12: Breeding your Dogo Argentino

Again, your Dogo Argentino may vomit and she may ask to go outside more frequently. Remember to stay with her when she goes to the bathroom to make sure a pup isn't born outside.

At this time, if the discharge turns to a dark green color, seek medical help. Dark green discharge is normal but only after a puppy is born. If it is before, it can indicate a life-threatening problem for both mother and litter.

Third Stage of Labor

This is the stage of labor when the puppies begin to be whelped. During this time, the contractions will become stronger and you will be able to see them. They will also occur closer together.

Your female Dogo Argentino may vomit during this time and you will notice that she will begin pushing and grunting. Some females will squat when they have their puppies, others will lie on their side so let the female decide how she is going to birth the puppy.

As she is pushing, you will see a membrane sac filled with water and the puppy come out of the vulva. Puppies are born in their own sac and it may burst while being delivered or as the female breaks it.

In addition, puppies are born both front feet first and breech position, with their tail or back feet presented first. The puppy is followed by the afterbirth. Females often eat the afterbirth as it contains material to stimulate milk production. Count each afterbirth after the puppies are born to make sure each one has been expelled. A retained afterbirth can cause a serious infection and lead to complications for your female.

Puppies are usually born in quick succession of two or three puppies. You will then have to wait about an hour or so before additional puppies are born.

The process of birthing can last up to 24 hours, depending on the size of the litter.

Chapter 12: Breeding your Dogo Argentino

If you find that the female is pushing for longer than 30 minutes without seeing a puppy, contact your veterinarian and follow his advice. It could mean a puppy is caught.

Also, if there is a long period of time between puppies, contact your veterinarian, especially if you are expecting more puppies.

When the puppies are born, allow them to nurse from their mother between births. Every time she is ready to push, remove the puppies to your basket. This keeps her from being distracted by the puppies and she is less likely to sit on the puppy or hurt it. Try to let her do the work herself. If you get too involved, you could cause her to stop laboring. Only get involved if she looks like she needs help.

In between puppies, weigh the puppy that was recently born, jot down all the notes on the puppy and place an identifier collar on the puppy.

Watching a litter being born is a very exciting thing but make sure you are prepared for any problems. Also, keep the whelping room quiet and calm.

It is also important to note that in the weeks after giving birth, the gland that is responsible for regulating the parathyroid hormone, which in turn regulates the amount of calcium, which is stored within the mother, can become depleted.

When the mother's milk starts to come in, and the demand for calcium suddenly is increased, the parathyroid gland is unable to respond quickly enough for her needs to be fully met. This can lead to her body contracting convulsively, which effectively will limit her movement. This condition is known as eclampsia.

Once diagnosed with eclampsia, the new mother will be prescribed calcium supplementation. Alternatively, foods such as Cottage Cheese, Goat's Milk, or Mature Cheddar will also help in supporting her to heal through this phase.

Chapter 12: Breeding your Dogo Argentino

If your female becomes fatigued during delivery or seems to be stalled, you can provide her with some vanilla ice cream for energy.

After whelping, be sure she eats and has plenty of fresh water. You can offer her some chicken or broth if her appetite is off. She should soon be hungry again since she will be nursing a litter of puppies.

Raising Pups

Raising pups is a fun activity and for the first few weeks, the mother does the majority of the work. She will clean the puppies and feed them. However, it doesn't mean that you have nothing to do - you will be very busy with your own chores. Below is a breakdown of what you need to do with the puppies while they are growing.

Puppy care & development tasks

Week 1

The puppies sleep the majority of the time. When they are awake, they will crawl towards warmth and milk. The puppies have their eyes and ears closed and are helpless at this age.

a) Chart weight twice a day.

b) Trim nails at the end of the week.

c) Handle the puppies daily to check their health and start neurological stimulation.

d) Clean the bedding daily.

e) Monitor the mother and her health.

f) Keep the whelping box temperature about 85°F (29.4°C).

Chapter 12: Breeding your Dogo Argentino

Week 2

Puppies are beginning to move around more and they are awake for longer periods.

a) Trim nails at the end of the week.

b) Hold the puppies in different positions to accustom them to being handled.

c) Monitor the mother and her health.

d) Clean bedding daily.

e) Weigh puppies once a day.

Eyes and ears

Eyes will begin to open at 8 - 10 days and ears will open near the end of week 2 or the start of week 3.

Week 3

Eyes and ears will be open by the end of this week and the pups will be more active.

They will start trying to walk and go to the bathroom without stimulation from mother. They will begin to play and their little teeth will be starting to show.

a) Continue to handle the puppies.

b) Trim nails at end of the week.

c) Begin getting the pups familiar with items such as grooming brushes and combs.

d) Weigh puppies every other day.

Chapter 12: Breeding your Dogo Argentino

e) Monitor the mother and her health.

f) Begin weaning process.

g) Start with milk replacer once a day for two days.

h) Then add a mushy food once per day.

i) Clean bedding daily.

Week 4

During this week, the puppies will be more playful and begin growling. They will also be eating mushy food and nurse occasionally.

Their mother will be resting more and feeding less, but should still be with them a lot. As soon as they start eating foods other than their mother's milk, cleaning up dog mess will be your job.

a) Continue to handle the puppies.

b) Trim nails at end of the week.

c) Begin familiarizing the puppies to other things such as noises and other animals in your home.

d) Weigh puppies every other day.

e) Monitor the mother and her health.

f) Shift the food to be the consistency of porridge and add one extra meal a day.

g) Clean bedding daily.

Chapter 12: Breeding your Dogo Argentino

Week 5

Puppies are more alert and they will be active. You will start to notice pack order and may even see sexual play. Puppies grow quickly during this time.

a) Weigh puppies two to three times each week.

b) Reduce the mother's diet to stop her milk production.

c) Start reducing the amount of liquid in the puppies' food.

d) Continue to handle the puppies.

e) Trim nails at end of the week.

f) Continue getting the puppies accustomed to a range of stimuli.

g) Clean bedding daily.

Week 6

Puppies are developing quickly and showing signs of their own personalities. Mother will spend less time with the puppies this stage.

a) Give each puppy time on their own.

b) Weigh the puppies weekly.

c) Continue reducing the amount of liquid in the puppies' food.

d) Continue to handle the puppies.

e) Trim nails at end of the week.

f) Continue widening the puppies' range of stimuli.

g) Clean bedding daily.

Chapter 12: Breeding your Dogo Argentino

Week 7

Puppies will be able to hear and see fully at this stage. They will be very inquisitive and can get into some problems if you just take your eyes off them for a second.

a) Give each puppy time alone.

b) Weigh the puppies weekly.

c) Puppies should be fully weaned and on puppy food.

d) Continue to handle the puppies.

e) Trim nails at end of the week.

f) Continue socializing the puppies to a range of stimuli.

g) Clean bedding daily.

Week 8

Puppies are at the age where they can start going to their new homes. This is the week when a fear period can occur so make sure you do not stress them too much.

a) Give each puppy some time alone.

b) Weigh the puppies weekly.

c) Trim nails at end of the week.

d) Continue socializing the puppies to a range of stimuli.

e) Clean bedding daily.

f) Start training puppies that have not already left for their new home.

Chapter 12: Breeding your Dogo Argentino

Note: Raising a litter of puppies is a lot of work so before you breed your Dogo Argentino, it's important to do a lot of research and be ready for the commitment. Any breeder will also tell you that it's advisable to have homes lined up for the puppies before you breed, or at least to know how you will place your puppies.

Dogo Argentino puppies may be highly desirable but it's still necessary to let people know you are breeding a litter. You will want to make sure your puppies are going to good homes after you have put so much work into breeding the litter and raising them. Most breeders have a waiting list and take deposits on their puppies when they are born.

Chapter 13: Saying Goodbye to your Dogo Argentino

Chapter Thirteen: Saying Goodbye to your Dogo Argentino

Chapter 13: Saying Goodbye to your Dogo Argentino

Saying goodbye to a beloved friend is never easy. That's true whether you have lived with your Dogo Argentino since he was a puppy or if you brought him home as an adult dog. It's easy to fall in love with a dog, especially a dog that devotes himself to you with love and affection.

One of the great drawbacks of having a pet is that we usually outlive them. Even if your dog lives to be 12 or 14 years old, there may come a time when you have to consider making a difficult decision.

In some cases an ageing dog will simply slip quietly away in his sleep or die suddenly. You may not have time to say goodbye or even to think about your dog's last days. But many dogs, as they grow older, will start to have a few nagging health problems. They will slow down, gain weight, and sleep more. You will notice their graying muzzle and perhaps signs of arthritis. All of these signs are indications that you should treasure every day with your dog because you may not have that much time left together.

Consider that the quality of life of the dog should always be the primary concern.

Vet care for older dogs

As your Dogo Argentino starts to grow older, you and your vet can begin to make some plans for him. By the time he is seven or eight years old, your veterinarian will probably suggest a senior exam for your dog. This involves some blood-work, urinalysis, and other tests so your vet will have some good baseline readings for your dog when he is young and healthy. Should your dog get sick, your vet will have a record of readings in order to make comparisons. Your vet will probably want to run the same kind of tests every year to see if there are any changes in your dog's health. This is a good way to catch any health problems early – before they become very serious.

You can also help with your older dog's care by checking him for lumps and bumps every time you groom him. Some fatty lumps and

Chapter 13: Saying Goodbye to your Dogo Argentino

other things are not unusual as a dog gets older, but you will still probably want your vet to look at any odd changes in your dog's skin or other changes that you notice. Finding a problem early means it can be removed or treated and your dog stands a much better chance of recovering.

Saying goodbye

Eventually, we all have to say goodbye to the dogs we love. If you are having a dog euthanized ("put to sleep"), it can help if you take a friend or a family member with you to the veterinarian's offices. This is a very emotional, difficult experience and emotional support can help you get through it. Some vets will come to your home to administer the injection which can be easier for your dog and you.

Some veterinarians can take care of a dog's remains but many owners prefer to do this. Depending on where you live, there are pet cemeteries and services that will cremate animals. Some owners find comfort in keeping their dog's ashes in an urn close by. In some rural areas it is common for owners to bury their dog on their own property.

Grief

Many pet owners suffer profound grief after the death of a pet. Unfortunately, they may have family and friends who do not understand their attachment to their pet. Many people have feelings for a pet like a member of the family. Losing that pet can be devastating. Going through grief surrounded by people who don't understand your loss can make your pain even worse.

If you are in this situation or feeling sad and depressed after losing your pet, there are support groups with other pet owners who understand how you feel. You can check online to find some of these groups and we will list some in the Resources section at the back of this book. You can also check your local newspapers and other local sources for support groups.

Chapter 13: Saying Goodbye to your Dogo Argentino

Many cities have pet-loss support groups. Even if your town doesn't have a group devoted to pet-loss, you can consider joining a group that discusses other kinds of loss, or talk to other pet owners who have also lost pets. They will understand what you are going through. You are definitely not alone.

Believe it or not, the feeling of loss will lessen and one day you will feel like having another dog again.

Chapter 14: Common Terms

Chapter Fourteen: Common Terms

So you are interested in the Dogo Argentino? While most of the vocabulary dealing with dogs is the same as with any other animal, there are a few terms that you should know.

In this chapter, we'll cover some common terms that you may encounter as you enjoy life with your Dogo Argentino.

Agility: is a sport in which the dog handler guides and instructs the dog through a course of obstacles while being timed. Accuracy through this obstacle course is paramount. The dogs must complete the obstacle course without a leash or toys (or food) as incentives. The handler can only use voice, movement and various body signals in order to direct the dog.

Acquired Immunity: when a dog has developed antibodies that enables it to resist a disease. Acquired Immunity is often seen in newborn puppies as they receive antibodies from their dam. It is also seen after vaccinations.

Chapter 14: Common Terms

Acute Disease: refers to a disease or illness that manifests quickly.

Adoption: to take an animal or person in as your own. Is commonly used to describe bringing in a dog from a shelter or rescue but can also be used when purchasing a puppy.

Afterbirth: is a term used to describe the fetal membranes and placenta that is expelled after the birth of a puppy.

Agent: a person who trains, works or shows a dog. Also known as a handler.

Albino: a genetic condition where an animal is born with white hair and pink eyes.

Allergen: a particle that triggers an allergic reaction. Found in dog hair, or specifically in a protein that is found in dog dander.

Almond eyes: eyes that have an elongated shape.

Alter: a term used to describe neutering or spaying.

Amble: used to describe a gait where the dog's legs on either side move almost as a pair.

Anal Glands: sacks or glands that are found on either side of the anus. All dogs use the substance secreted by the gland to mark territory.

Anestrus: the period of time between heats in female dogs.

Ankle: found in the hind legs, it is the area between the second thigh and metatarsus where there is a collection of bones. Also known as the hock.

Anterior: the front of the dog.

Apron: refers to longer hair on the chest, also known as the frill.

Chapter 14: Common Terms

Arm: refers to the area between the shoulder and elbow of the dog's front legs.

Articulation: refers to the area where bones meet.

Artificial Insemination: used during breeding, it refers to using artificial means to place semen into the bitch's reproductive tract.

Asymptomatic: when a dog has a disease but is not exhibiting symptoms.

Awn hairs: seen on dogs with double coats, it is the section of undercoat that is long and has a coarse texture to it. It should be slightly longer than the downy undercoat but shorter than the outer coat.

Assertion: when a dog has more assertive characteristics than other dogs

Back: the area on the dog that extends from the shoulders to the rump of the dog.

Back crossing: refers to the act of breeding a dog to its parent.

<u>It not recommended to do this. The coefficient of inbreeding should be as low as possible.</u>

Backyard Breeder: a term that refers to a breeder that breeds dogs for profit with little care for the health of the dogs and puppies.

Bad Mouth: when a dog has crooked teeth.

Balance: used to describe the symmetry of the dog as well as its proportion.

Bandy Legs: refers to legs that bend outward.

Barrel: refers to the area around the ribs of a dog.

Chapter 14: Common Terms

Barrel Hocks: also known as spread hocks, refers to legs where the hock turns outward, which makes the feet turn inward.

Beefy: when a dog has too much weight in his hindquarters.

Behavior Modification: using training and conditioning to control, alter or teach specific behaviors. Usually refers to aggression, fear and reactivity.

Bitch: a common term used to describe a female dog.

Bite: when a dog places his teeth on something. Also used to describe the position of the upper and lower teeth when the dog has his mouth closed.

Blocky: when the dog has a square like shape to his head.

Blooded: refers to a dog with a pedigree that comes from a good breeding.

Bloodline: the pedigree of the dog.

Blunt Muzzle: when a dog has a square shaped muzzle.

Board: when the dog is placed in a location where the care, feeding and housing of the dog is paid for. Usually used when owners are on vacation.

Body Length: measured from the front of the breastbone to the pelvis to identify how long a dog is.

Booster Vaccination: injections given to a dog to boost the immunity they have to specific diseases. Usually given on a yearly basis.

Bossy: when a dog has shoulder muscles that have been over developed.

Chapter 14: Common Terms

Brace: refers to two dogs that are presented as a pair. They should be of the same breed.

Break: when there is a change in coloration between the puppy and adult coat.

Breastbone: the area on the chest where 8 bones connect to form the area.

Breech Birth: the presentation of the puppy at birth. In breech, the puppy comes out hind end first. Breech birth is very common in dogs and does not usually cause a problem.

Breeches: fur on the upper thighs that is longer and fringe like. Also known as pants, culottes and trousers.

Breed: refers to a group of dogs that share common characteristics, traits and gene pool.

Breed Club: refers to a group of enthusiasts dedicated to a specific breed.

Breeder: Any person who produces a litter or breeds a dog.

Breed Rescue: a rescue group that specialized in finding homes for unwanted dogs of a specific breed.

Breed Standard: a description of a breed that describes the physical characteristics as well as temperament to expect in a set breed.

Breeding Particulars: the information about a breeding or litter such as the parents, sex and color of the puppy and the date of birth.

Brick Shaped: a dog that has a rectangular shape.

Brisket: usually refers to the breastbone or sternum. However, it can also refer to the entire chest and thorax of the dog.

Chapter 14: Common Terms

Brood Bitch: used to refer to a female dog that has or will be used for breeding.

Brows: the ridge above the eye.

Brush: when a tail has a heavy amount of hair on it.

Brushing: refers to a gait where the dog's legs brush against each other when he walks.

Butterfly: refers to a nose that has only a small or partial amount of pigmentation on it.

Buttocks: the rump of the dog.

By-products: found in food labels, it refers to any food that is not suitable for human consumption.

Camel Back: a dog that has an arched back.

Canid: refers to any animal in the canidae family such as dogs, wolves and foxes.

Canine: a term for dog.

Canine Teeth: also known as eye teeth, the largest teeth found in the dog's mouth. They are long, curved teeth on either side of the mouth, top and bottom.

Canter: a run where the dog has three beats.

Cape: refers to longer hair over the shoulders.

Carnivore: an animal that eats only the flesh of other animals.

Carpals: the bones found in the wrist.

Carrier: when a dog carries a disease that it can transmit to other animals without showing any signs of the disease.

Chapter 14: Common Terms

Castrate: when the dog's testicles are removed.

Cat Foot: refers to a foot that is round with high-arched toes.

Cheek: the area between the lips and front of ears just under the eyes.

Chest: the area around the ribs.

Chippendale Front: when the dog's forelegs push out at the elbows on the front legs and the feet turn out.

Chiseled: a dog with a head free of bumps and bulges.

Chronic Disease: refers to a disease that will last indefinitely.

Cleft Palate: when the two halves of the mouth do not fuse properly. It is a birth defect.

Clipping: When a dog's back foot hits the front foot when walking.

Cloddy: a dog that is thick and heavy.

Close Mating: used to describe the act of breeding the same female shortly after her previous litter was whelped. The period of time would be less than 4 months and 15 days.

Close Coupled: refers to a short length of body between the last set of ribs and the hind quarters.

Coarse: a dog that is not refined. Also refers to the texture of the coat when it has a hard or rough texture.

Coat: the fur that covers the dog.

Cobby: a dog with a short body.

Colostrum: the clear to yellowish milk produced by a dam during the first 48 hours after her puppies are born.

Chapter 14: Common Terms

Concaveation: when a spayed female produces milk.

Condition: the overall look and health of the dog.

Conformation: a term used to describe the physical traits of a breed.

Congenital: a disease or condition that is present at birth. Congenital problems are not necessarily hereditary.

Coupling: refers to the part of the dog's body that is between the ribs and hind quarters.

Cow-hocked: when the dog's hocks turn inward and cause the feet to turn outward.

Crate: Also known as a kennel, the crate is a container that is used for housing dogs.

Crest: the area on the neck that is arched.

Crossbred: when a dog has a dam and sire from different breeds. Also known as a cur.

Croup: the area around the pelvic girdle.

Crown: the top of the head.

Culottes: fur on the upper thighs that is longer and fringe like. Also known as pants, breeches and trousers.

Cur: when a dog has a dam and sire from different breeds. Also known as a crossbreed or mutt.

Cynology: the study of dogs and canines.

Dam: a female dog that is pregnant or has puppies. Also refers to the female parent or mother.

Dander: the skin that is sloughed off of the dog.

Chapter 14: Common Terms

Date of Whelping: refers to the date when the puppies are born.

Dealer: an individual who buys puppies from a breeder and then sells the puppies to others. It is recommended that you avoid puppy dealers.

Deep Chest: A dog or dog breed that has a longer chest or rib cage.

Dentition: the number of teeth in an adult dog, which is 42.

Dewclaw: the claw that is found on the inside of the leg above the foot.

Digit: refers to a toe.

Dock: the act of cutting a dog's tail short.

Dog: refers to canines, however, it is also the term used for a male canine.

Domed Skull: a skull that is rounded.

Domesticated: a term used to describe any animal that has been tamed.

Double coat: refers to a type of dog coat that has two coats; the soft undercoat that provides warmth and the topcoat that provides protection from the weather and terrain.

Down Hairs: the shortest hairs on a dog, which is usually soft and downy in texture.

Dudley Nose: a nose that has no pigmentation.

Elbow: the area on the posterior of the forearm.

Elbows Out: when a dog's elbows turn away from the body.

Embryo: a term used to describe an undeveloped fetus.

Entire: a dog that has not been altered and its reproductive system is complete. Also called intact.

Chapter 14: Common Terms

Estrus: the period of a dog's heat cycle when the female is most receptive to being mated. It precedes ovulation.

Euthanasia: the practice of ending life through medical means.

Even Bite: when the lower and upper incisors have no overlap.

Expression: the features of the head and how they look.

F1: the offspring of a direct crossing of two purebred dogs.

F2: the offspring of one F1 parent and one purebred parent. Could also refer to the offspring of two F1 parents.

F3: the offspring of one F1 parent and one F2 parent. Could also refer to the offspring of two F2 parents.

Fang: the canines.

Feathering: Long hair on the ears, tail, legs or body that has a fringe like appearance.

Feral: a dog that has returned to a wild state.

Fetus: the unborn puppy.

Fever: an indication that there is an illness. The body temperature rises to over 103°F in dogs.

Fiddle Front: when a dog's elbows and feet turn out but the pasterns are close together.

Fillers: found in dog food, it is a chemical or low quality, indigestible food that adds weight to the dog food.

Fixed: a term to describe a dog that has been neutered or spayed.

Flank: the side of a dog's body that is between the hip and last rib.

Chapter 14: Common Terms

Flat-Sided: a dog that has flat rib, the desired shape is rounded. Sometimes called slab-sided.

Floating Rib: in dogs, the 13th rib is not attached to the other ribs.

Flying Trot: a run where all four of the dog's feet are off the ground for a second on each half stride.

Foster Mother: a female dog that is nursing puppies that are not her own.

Fresh Extended Semen: this is used in artificial insemination breeding where semen is extracted from a male dog and an extender is placed in the semen to expand the lifespan of the semen.

Frill: refers to longer hair on the chest, also known as the apron.

Front: the part of the dog's body that is in the front. This is the forelegs, shoulder line, chest, head, etc.

Frozen Semen: used in artificial insemination breeding, it is semen that is extracted from the male dog and frozen to be used at a later date.

Furrow: an indentation found in the centre of the skull to the stop at the dog's muzzle.

Gait: the pattern of steps when a dog is in movement.

Gallop: when the dog is running.

Gaskin: the lower thigh on the dog.

Genetically Linked Defects: health problems that are passed from parent to offspring.

Gestation Period: used in breeding, it is the time period between mating and birth.

Chapter 14: Common Terms

Get: the offspring of a dog.

Groom: brushing, bathing, trimming and caring for the hygienic needs of the dog's coat.

Guard Hairs: the hair that are stiffer and longer than the other hair. Usually protects the dog from the terrain and weather.

Hackles: the hairs found on the back of a dog's neck. It will stand up when the dog is angry or frightened.

Handler: a person who trains, works or shows a dog, also known as an agent.

Haunch Bones: term referring to the hip bones.

Haw: the third eyelid found in dogs.

Head: this is used to describe the front portion of the dog, which includes the muzzle, face, ears and cranium.

Heat: when a dog begins to produce a blood like discharge from her vulva to signal that she is starting her estrus cycle.

Height: height is always measured from the bottom of the foot (ground) to the tallest point on the withers (shoulders).

High in Rear: a dog that has a back end that is higher than its shoulders.

Hock: found in the hind legs, it is the area between the second thigh and metatarsus where there is a collection of bones, also known as the ankle.

Housebreak: training a puppy not to defecate or urinate in the house.

Immunization: when shots are given to a dog to help produce immunity to a specific disease.

Chapter 14: Common Terms

Imported Semen: when frozen semen is imported from another country.

In and In: refers to any form of inbreeding in dogs where little consideration is given to the results.

Inbreeding: mating two dogs that are closely related. These include mother to son, daughter to son, sibling to sibling.

Incisors: the upper and lower teeth found at the front of the mouth between the canines. Adult dogs have six upper and six lower.

Incubation Period: the period of time between being infected with a disease and the first symptom appearing.

Interbreeding: breeding dogs that are of different breeds. Also called cross-breeding.

Jacobsen's Organ: this is an organ located in the dog's mouth, specifically on the roof, that functions as a sensory organ for taste and smell.

Keel: the rounded area of the chest.

Kennel: Also known as a crate, the kennel is a container that is used for housing dogs. Also used to describe a place that houses and/or breeds dogs. Many breeders use the term loosely to describe a line of dogs, i.e. "Her kennel produces lovely dogs."

Knuckling Over: a condition seen primarily in puppies where the wrist joints flex forward when the dog is standing.

Lactation: the milk that is produced by the mammary glands from a female dog.

Lead: a term used to describe a leash.

Leather: the part of the outer ear that is supported by cartilage.

Chapter 14: Common Terms

Line: the pedigree or family of dogs that are related.

Line Breeding: when a dog is bred to another member of its bloodline such as grandfather to granddaughter, aunt to nephew, uncle to niece.

Litter: the puppies that are produced during a whelping. It can refer to one puppy or several.

Litter Complement: refers to the number of puppies of each sex in a litter.

Litter Registration: a record with a kennel club of a litter.

Lumbering: refers to a dog with a gait that is awkward.

Mad Dog: refers to a dog that has rabies.

Marking: a behavior done primarily by males, although it can be seen in females, where a dog will urinate to establish the boundaries of its territory.

Markings: used to describe the patterns found on a dog's coat.

Mask: when there is dark shading on the face.

Mate: when a male dog and female dog are bred.

Maternal Immunity: seen in newborn puppies, it is a resistance to disease that is temporarily passed from mother to pup.

Measure Out: when a dog's height is larger than the breed standard.

Microchip: a small chip that is inserted under the skin. It contains a code that can be scanned and all the owner's information for the dog can be pulled up. Used as identification.

Milk Teeth: the puppy's first teeth, which will fall out to make way for adult teeth during the first year of life.

Chapter 14: Common Terms

Molars: the square, posterior teeth that is used for chewing.

Mongrel: when a dog has a dam and sire from different breeds, also known as a crossbreed.

Monorchid: a dog that only has one testicle.

Muzzle: the protruding section of the dog's head which includes the mouth, and nose.

Natural Breed: a breed of dog that developed without human interference. Sometimes called a landrace breed.

Nesting Behavior: seen in pregnant female dogs or those going through a false pregnancy. It is when the bitch prepares a place to whelp her young.

Neuter: when the dog's testicles are removed.

Nick: refers to a breeding between dogs of two different bloodlines that consistently produces puppies that are desirable according to the breed standard.

Nictitating Membrane: the third eyelid found in dogs.

Odd-Eyed: when one eye is a different color than the other.

Omnivore: an animal that eats both animal flesh and vegetation.

On-Dog Identification: any form of identification that enables people to identify the dog.

Outcrossing: breeding two dogs that are not related but are still of the same breed.

Overage Dam: an older dam that is older than 7 years old when she is bred.

Chapter 14: Common Terms

Overage Sire: an older sire that is older than 12 years old when he is bred.

Overhang: a dog with an overly pronounced brow.

Overshot: when the upper jaw protrudes out and the lower jaw is behind the upper jaw when the mouth is closed.

Ovulate: when the ovary releases a mature ovum.

Pants: fur on the upper thighs that is longer and fringe like, also known as breeches, culottes and trousers.

Pedigree: a record of a dog's genealogy.

Pen Breeding: when a breeding occurs due to a male and female dog being penned together. The breeding is not witnessed.

Pile: the dense and soft hair that is the undercoat.

Pinking Up: used to describe a pregnant female dog when her nipples begin to turn pink.

Plucking: the act of pulling out loose hair by hand. Some breeds need to be hand-groomed by plucking.

Purebred: a dog that has parents, grandparents and so on of the same breed.

Quick: the vein that is found in the dog's nail.

Registration Papers: documents from a registry that show proof of breed and whether the dog is purebred.

Scent: the odor that is left in the air or on the ground by an animal.

Scissors Bite: when the lower incisors touch the upper incisors when the dog's mouth is closed.

Chapter 14: Common Terms

Season: refers to the period of time when the female dog can be bred.

Secondary Coat: the hairs that are found in the undercoat.

Selective Breeding: when a breeder chooses to breed two dogs together in the hopes of eliminating or achieving a trait.

Septum: the line that is seen between the two nostrils of the dog.

Service Dog: a specially trained dog that works with people who have disabilities.

Show Quality: a dog that is an excellent representation of the breed standard.

Silent Heat: when a female dog goes into heat but shows little or no outward signs that she is in heat.

Single Coat: a dog that does not have an undercoat.

Sire: the male dog, specifically the male parent.

Smooth Coat: a short coat, close to the body.

Soundness: a dog that has both mental and physical health functioning properly.

Spay: a procedure where the reproductive organs of a female are removed. This prevents heat and the female from becoming pregnant.

Spectacles: when there are dark markings around the eyes.

Spread Hock: refers to legs where the hock turns outward, which makes the feet turn inward, also known as barrel hocks.

Stacking: the way a dog stands when being exhibited in a dog show.

Standing Heat: the period during heat when the female will accept a male and can become pregnant.

Chapter 14: Common Terms

Stray Dog: a dog that is lost or homeless.

Teat: the nipple of an animal.

Topcoat: the hair that is stiffer and longer than the others. Usually protects the dog from the terrain and weather.

Trousers: fur on the upper thighs that is longer and fringe like, also known as pants, culottes and breeches.

Tuck Up: the waist of the dog where the body is shallower in depth.

Typey: a dog that exhibits the conformation of the breed standard.

Underage Dam: a female dog that is bred before she is 8 months of age.

Underage Sire: a male dog that is bred before he is 7 months of age.

Undershot: when the lower jaw protrudes past the upper jaw while the mouth is closed.

Unsound: refers to a dog that is physically or mentally unable to perform in the way it was intended.

Vaccine: a shot that is given to a dog to help produce immunity to a specific disease.

Variety: when one breed has several subtypes, such as long haired and short haired, but both subtypes can be interbred.

Vent: the anus or anal opening.

Wean: the process of switching a puppy from milk to solid foods.

Weedy: a dog that lacks the musculature that is described in the standard.

Whelp Date: the date when the litter is born.

Chapter 14: Common Terms

Whelping: this is the term used to describe a dam giving birth.

Withers: the top of the shoulders of the dog.

Zoonosis: a disease that can be passed from animal to human.

Chapter 15: Resources

Chapter Fifteen: Resources

Now that you know everything you can about the Dogo Argentino, here are some resources that will help make owning your Dogo Argentino easier. These are both specific breed resources for the Dogo Argentino and general dog resources.

Dogo Argentino Resources

The first resources that you should have on hand are those related directly to your Dogo Argentino. Some excellent ones to start with are:

AKC Meet The Breeds: Dogo Argentino

http://www.akc.org/breeds/argentine_dogo/index.cfm

Dogo Argentino Club of America

Chapter 15: Resources

http://www.dogousa.org/

Canadian Dogo Argentino Club

http://www.dogoargentinocanada.com/

Dog Breed Info: Dogo Argentino

http://www.dogbreedinfo.com/dogo.htm

Dog Breeds of the World: Dogo Argentino

http://www.bulldoginformation.com/dogo-argentino-bloodlines.html

Dogo Argentino Information

http://dogobreeder.blogspot.ca/2010/04/how-to-train-my-dogo-for-big-game.html

Federation Cynologique Internationale: Dogo Argentino

http://www.fci.be/Nomenclature/Standards/292g02-en.pdf

Chapter 15: Resources

Dogo Argentino Breeders

It is not always easy to find Dogo Argentino breeders. Even some of the parent clubs for this breed do not currently list any breeders. Here are some breeders with web sites online. We are not necessarily recommending these breeders but you can visit their sites to see their photos and find out if they have litters planned. As always, please investigate any breeder in whom you are interested.

La Cocha Kennel, Argentina; the family of Dr. Nores Martinez, creator of the breed

http://www.dogoargentinonores.com/

Massimo Inzoli, Italy

http://www.dogoargentino.it/about_us.asp

Katana Caza Mayor, Japan

http://www.dogoargentino-japan.com/

Dogoman's De Calfucura

http://dogoman.com.ar/

Valiente Dogo, Quebec, Canada

www.valientedogo.com

Torrida Dogos, Quebec, Canada

www.torridadogos.com

Stoneham Dogos, Ontario, Canada

Chapter 15: Resources

www.stonhamsdogos.com

Milcayac Dogos, Ontario, Canada

www.milcayacdogos.com

Del Immortal Dogo Argentino, Alberta, Canada

www.truedogos.com

Los Polleo, Ohio, USA

http://dogwebs.net/lospolleo/

El Toro Dogos

http://eltorodogos.com

La Historia

www.argentine-dogo.com

Mistymoor kennel

www.mistymoorkennel.com

Las Pampas Kennels, United States

www.dogoargentino.com

Southern Dogos, Louisiana, USA

www.southerndogos.com

Chapter 15: Resources

Dog Owner Resources

Finally, here are a few dog owner resources that will help you navigate your way through pet ownership. It is important to note that we are not affiliated with any of these sites. Always discuss your dog's health and training issues with trained professionals.

AltVetMed: http://www.altvetmed.org/

Association of Professional Dog Trainers: APDT.com

American College of Veterinary Nutrition: http://www.acvn.org/

American Dog Trainers Network: http://www.inch.com/~dogs/

Breeder.net: http://www.breeders.net/

Behavior Adjustment Training: www.empoweredanimals.com

Canine Eye Registration Foundation: http://web.vmdb.org/home/CERF.aspx

Canine Health Foundation: http://www.akcchf.org/

DogAware: http://dogaware.com/

Canine Health Information Center: http://www.caninehealthinfo.org/

Certification Council for Professional Dog Trainers: http://www.ccpdt.org

David Mech (Recantation of Dominance Theory): http://www.davemech.org/news.html

Dog Food Advisor: www.dogfoodadvisor.com

Chapter 15: Resources

DogAware: http://dogaware.com/

DogFood.guru

Dog Owners' Guide: http://www.canismajor.com/

Dog Time: http://dogtime.com/

Dr. Jean Dodds Vaccination Protocol: http://www.weim.net/emberweims/Vaccine.html

Dr. Foster and Smith Pet Education: http://www.peteducation.com/

Dr Sophia Yin (Further debunking of dominance and pack theories): http://drsophiayin.com/philosophy/dominance

Healthy Pet: http://www.aaha.org/pet_owner/

International Association of Animal Behavior Consultants: https://iaabc.org

Medline Plus: http://www.nlm.nih.gov/medlineplus/pethealth.html

Orthopedic Foundation for Animals: http://www.offa.org/

PAW: http://www.paw-rescue.org/

Pet Diets: https://www.petdiets.com/

Pet Loss: http://www.petloss.com/

Pet-Loss Support: http://www.pet-loss.net/

PetMD: http://www.petmd.com/

Pet Pharmacy: http://www.veterinarypartner.com

Chapter 15: Resources

Pet Professional Guild: http://www.petprofessionalguild.com

Petstyle: http://www.petstyle.com/

Rainbow Bridge Pet Loss: https://rainbowsbridge.com/

Suzanne Clothier, Myth of Reinforcing Fear:

http://fearfuldogs.com/myth-of-reinforcing-fear/

Terrific Pets: http://www.terrificpets.com/

VetInfo: http://www.vetinfo.com/

Vetmedicine: http://vetmedicine.about.com/

Vetquest: http://www.vetquest.com/

Whole Pet: http://www.wholepetvet.com/

Chapter 15: Resources

Photo Credits

Front Cover Photo by: Michal Slepanek

Back Cover Photo by: Sophie Desbiens

Dr Agustin Nores Martinez Quote Page Photo by: Josip Lucin

Chapter 1 Photo by: Michal Slepanek

Chapter 2 Photo by: Michal Slepanek

Chapter 3 Photo by Josip Lucin

Chapter 4 Photo by: Michal Slepanek

Chapter 5 Photo by Josip Lucin

Chapter 6 Photo by Josip Lucin

Chapter 7 Photo by: Michal Slepanek

Chapter 8 Photo by Josip Lucin

Chapter 9 Photo by Josip Lucin

Chapter 10 Photo by Josip Lucin

Chapter 11 Photo by: Michal Slepanek

Chapter 12 Photo by Josip Lucin

Chapter 13 Photo by Josip Lucin

Chapter 14 Photo by Josip Lucin

Chapter 15 Photo by Josip Lucin

It was a pleasure working with you all. Thank you.